Quick & Easy
Low-Carb Cooking

For people with diabetes

Nancy S. Hughes

▲.American Diabetes Association.

*Cure • Care • Commitment*SM

Director, Book Publishing, John Fedor; *Associate Director, Consumer Books,* Sherrye Landrum; *Editor,* Laurie Guffey; *Associate Director, Book Production,* Peggy M. Rote; *Composition,* Circle Graphics; *Cover Design,* Koncept Inc; *Printer,* United Graphics, Inc.

Printed in the United States of America
3 5 7 9 10 8 6 4 2

The suggestions and information contained in this publication are generally consistent with the *Clinical Practice Recommendations* and other policies of the American Diabetes Association, but they do not represent the policy or position of the Association or any of its boards or committees. Reasonable steps have been taken to ensure the accuracy of the information presented. However, the American Diabetes Association cannot ensure the safety or efficacy of any product or service described in this publication. Individuals are advised to consult a physician or other appropriate health care professional before undertaking any diet or exercise program or taking any medication referred to in this publication. Professionals must use and apply their own professional judgment, experience, and training and should not rely solely on the information contained in this publication before prescribing any diet, exercise, or medication. The American Diabetes Association—its officers, directors, employees, volunteers, and members—assumes no responsibility or liability for personal or other injury, loss, or damage that may result from the suggestions or information in this publication.

♾ The paper in this publication meets the requirements of the ANSI Standard Z39.48-1992 (permanence of paper).

ADA titles may be purchased for business or promotional use or for special sales. To purchase this book in large quantities, or for custom editions of this book with your logo, contact Lee Romano Sequeira, Special Sales & Promotions, at the address below, or at LRomano@diabetes.org or 703-299-2046.

American Diabetes Association
1701 North Beauregard Street
Alexandria, Virginia 22311

Library of Congress Cataloging-in-Publication Data

Hughes, Nancy S.
    Quick & easy low-carb cooking for people with diabetes / Nancy S. Hughes.
      p. cm.
    Includes index.
    ISBN 1-58040-147-3 (pbk. : alk. paper)
    1. Diabetes—Diet therapy—Recipes. 2. Low-carbohydrate diet—Recipes. 3. Quick and easy cookery. I. Title: Quick and easy low-carb cooking for people with diabetes. II. Title.

RC662.H843 2003
641.5'6314—dc21   2003056070

Dedication

To my husband, Greg,
whose sense of humor and crooked grin
always gives me instant peace when I'm cross-eyed.

To my son, Will, 27, and my new daughter, Kelly, 25,
whose sweet, quiet contentment has a way of spilling over
and calming me down when I'm "red-lining."

To my daughter, Annie, 24,
for giving me the "show-how" to handle those long, long days
and even longer nights, sympathizing profusely whenever I ask for it.

To my son, Taft, 19,
for helping me through the computer glitches
and giving me those "get a grip" looks when I'm teetering.

Stay close to me, family . . . I need you—as you can obviously see!

Contents

Acknowledgments

Thanks to some very special editors, Sherrye Landrum and Laurie Guffey, for inviting me into your world and giving me the freedom to be creative, the boundaries in which to work, and the opportunity to acquire an unexpected wealth of information. You made a very hard subject simple enough that even I could understand it.

Thanks to Sarees Zieman: my right hand, my left hand, and oftentimes, my sentence finisher . . . thank you for knowing what's needed and when, especially when I don't.

And finally, thanks to David Hughes, my brother-in-law, who makes my spirits and energy soar every time we talk . . . thanks for believing in me so much, David.

Introduction

I'm tired of keeping track of all these numbers! Carb and fat grams, blood glucose, calories . . . all these numbers can be a real pain. I'm a mother of three, a wife, and a career woman . . . a quick night's sleep and two or three mini moments are sometimes the only stops I make in the course of a 24-hour day. So what I do with my time is important, as it is to all of us . . . but even more important is keeping blood glucose levels on target and carb intake consistent. When I don't overload on carbs, I have more energy, my mind is clearer, I don't have those pesky highs and lows, and I don't have the undermining, underlying craving for something to munch on . . . all the time! The closer I get to the end of the day, though, the faster I seem to run, and the more I don't want to cook . . . especially if there's food math involved!

So, to make things easier for all of us, I've written this book. You can throw your calculator in a drawer, because I've done the homework for you. I've kept the ingredient list short (most recipes have 6–8 ingredients) and the prep time shorter (less than 30 minutes). Best of all, I suggest accompaniments for every recipe so you can serve quick, complete meals . . . and I tell you exactly how many carb grams are in each recipe and meal, thus eliminating the need for any calculations on your part!

The book is divided into sections with quick snacks, breakfasts, lunches, dinners, and desserts that provide 1, 2, 3, 4, or 5 carb choices (or carb exchanges) for the entire meal. The "Try it with" section tells you what you can serve with that recipe. The carb exchange total given in that section is for the recipe plus the "Try it with" items. If you want to serve the recipe by itself or with other side dishes but you still need the recipe's carb grams, look in the nutritional analysis section.

There is only one recipe per meal to follow . . . the sides can be thrown in the microwave, quickly steamed, or simply tossed with dressing to round out the meal. I always try to use the freshest and simplest ingredients available. And when I call for margarine, know that of the four general margarine categories—regular, about 70% fat, about 35%

fat, and fat-free—I use the 35% fat variety and that's how the recipes were analyzed.

As in my previous book, *Last Minute Meals for People with Diabetes,* these recipes are geared for the real (that is, busy) lives that we all lead. My family loves these recipes . . . and I love getting in and out of the kitchen in a flash!

SNACKS

1

Carb Exchange

Cheesy Tortilla Rollers

4 soft corn tortillas
1 teaspoon ground cumin
1/2 teaspoon dried red pepper flakes
4 (3/4-ounce) cheddar and mozzarella blend
  cheese sticks

1 Place tortillas on a work surface. Sprinkle each tortilla evenly with 1/4 teaspoon cumin and 1/8 teaspoon dried pepper flakes. Place a cheese stick in the center of each tortilla, roll tortilla around cheese, and place seam side down on a microwave-safe plate.

2 Place in microwave and cook on HIGH setting 30–45 seconds or until cheese is just beginning to melt.

3 Remove from microwave and let stand 30 seconds to cool slightly for easier handling.

Exchanges
1 Starch
1 Medium-Fat Meat

Calories....................135
  Calories from Fat......70
Total Fat........................8 g
  Saturated Fat...............4 g
Cholesterol.................20 mg
Sodium.....................370 mg
Carbohydrate............12 g
  Dietary Fiber................1 g
  Sugars...........................0 g
Protein..........................5 g

Crostini with Herbed Balsamic Oil

    8 ounces baguette-style French bread
    2 tablespoons extra virgin olive oil
    1 tablespoon balsamic vinegar
    1 tablespoon water
  1/2 medium garlic clove, minced
    2 teaspoons dried basil leaves
  3/4 teaspoon dried oregano leaves
  1/4 teaspoon dried rosemary leaves
  1/4 teaspoon black pepper
  1/8 teaspoon salt

1 Preheat oven to 350°F.

2 Cut bread into 24 1/2-inch-wide slices and place on cookie sheet. Bake 13 minutes or until just beginning to brown lightly.

3 Remove from heat and let cool completely.

4 In a jar, combine remaining ingredients, secure with a tight lid, and shake vigorously.

5 Brush slices of bread with herb mixture.

Exchanges
1 Starch
1/2 Fat

Calories 101
  Calories from Fat 31
Total Fat .... 3 g
  Saturated Fat .... 0 g
Cholesterol .... 0 mg
Sodium .... 208 mg
Carbohydrate .... 15 g
  Dietary Fiber .... 1 g
  Sugars .... 0 g
Protein .... 3 g

Mediterranean Morsels

12 green olives stuffed with pimiento, drained
 5 ounces cherry tomatoes, preferably sweet grape
   variety, rinsed and patted dry
 1 14-ounce can cut hearts of palm, drained
 4 ounces small or large whole mushrooms,
   quartered
1/2 cup canned garbanzo beans, rinsed and drained
1 1/2 tablespoons extra virgin olive oil
 1 tablespoon dried basil leaves
20 plain crisp breadsticks (4 × 1/2 inches)

1 Combine all ingredients except breadsticks in a
gallon-sized plastic storage bag. Seal tightly and
shake gently back and forth to coat completely.

2 Refrigerate 4 hours to allow flavors to blend.
Serve with breadsticks and wooden toothpicks.

Exchanges

1/2 Starch
1 Vegetable
1/2 Fat

Calories 94
  Calories from Fat 37
Total Fat .... 4 g
  Saturated Fat ....0 g
Cholesterol ....0 mg
Sodium ....295 mg
Carbohydrate .... 12 g
  Dietary Fiber ....2 g
  Sugars ....2 g
Protein .... 3 g

Veggie Dippers

      1 cup fat-free sour cream
1 1/2 tablespoons dried dill weed
      1 tablespoon plus 1 teaspoon extra virgin olive oil
      2 teaspoons lime juice
      1 teaspoon Dijon mustard
   1/2 teaspoon salt
   1/4 teaspoon hot pepper sauce
2 1/2 cups cucumber slices

Place all ingredients except cucumber slices in a small mixing bowl and stir until well blended. Serve with cucumber slices.

Exchanges

1/2 Fat
1 Carbohydrate

Calories	84
Calories from Fat	34
Total Fat	4 g
Saturated Fat	0 g
Cholesterol	3 mg
Sodium	319 mg
Carbohydrate	10 g
Dietary Fiber	1 g
Sugars	4 g
Protein	2 g

Pepperoni-Jalapeño Melts

12 low-sodium Triscuit-style crackers
 6 turkey pepperoni slices, halved
 2 jalapeño chili peppers, each cut in 6 slices
   crosswise
1/4 cup shredded reduced-fat sharp cheddar cheese

1 Place crackers in a single layer on a microwave-safe plate. Top each cracker with 1 pepperoni slice and 1 jalapeño slice. Sprinkle cheese evenly over all.

2 Cook in microwave on HIGH setting 15 seconds or until cheese just begins to melt.

Exchanges
1/2 Starch
1 Fat

Calories 88
   Calories from Fat 38
Total Fat ....4 g
   Saturated Fat ....1 g
Cholesterol ....9 mg
Sodium ....148 mg
Carbohydrate ....10 g
   Dietary Fiber ....2 g
   Sugars ....0 g
Protein ....4 g

On-a-Budget Brown Bag Popcorn

Serves: 2

Serving size:
 2 1/2 cups

1/4 cup popcorn kernels
  1 brown paper sandwich bag
30 pumps butter spray
1/8 teaspoon salt

1 Place popcorn in paper bag, fold edges over twice to seal, place in microwave, and cook on popcorn setting.

2 Remove bag from microwave, spray popcorn 10 times with butter spray, seal bag, and shake. Repeat 2 times, add salt, and shake vigorously to coat completely.

Exchanges

1 Starch
1 Fat

Calories......................111
  Calories from Fat......44
Total Fat........................5 g
  Saturated Fat...............0 g
Cholesterol...................0 mg
Sodium.....................152 mg
Carbohydrate............16 g
  Dietary Fiber...............3 g
  Sugars...........................0 g
Protein..........................2 g

Peach Fizz Smoothie

1 cup reduced-fat artificially sweetened
   vanilla ice cream
1 cup frozen unsweetened peach slices
1 12-ounce can diet ginger ale
1 1/2 tablespoons sugar
1 teaspoon vanilla

Blend all ingredients until smooth.

Exchanges
1 Carbohydrate

Calories 83
   Calories from Fat 21
Total Fat .... 2 g
   Saturated Fat .... 1 g
Cholesterol .... 13 mg
Sodium .... 42 mg
Carbohydrate .... 14 g
   Dietary Fiber .... 1 g
   Sugars .... 11 g
Protein .... 2 g

SNACKS

2

Carb Exchanges

White Bean and Sweet Red Pepper Salsa with Pita Wedges

3 6-inch pita breads, each cut in half
3/4 cup canned navy beans, rinsed and drained
1 medium red bell pepper, finely chopped
2 tablespoons lemon juice
1 tablespoon extra virgin olive oil
1 tablespoon capers, drained
1/2 teaspoon dried oregano leaves
1/2 medium garlic clove, minced

1 Preheat oven to 350°F.

2 Cut each pita half into 6 wedges. Place on a baking sheet and bake 5 minutes or until just beginning to brown lightly. Cool completely.

3 Meanwhile, combine remaining ingredients in a medium mixing bowl and toss gently, yet thoroughly. Serve with pita wedges.

Exchanges
2 Starch

Calories 145
   Calories from Fat 25
Total Fat .... 3 g
   Saturated Fat .... 0 g
Cholesterol .... 0 mg
Sodium .... 257 mg
Carbohydrate .... 25 g
   Dietary Fiber .... 3 g
   Sugars .... 2 g
Protein .... 5 g

Pears with Cinnamon Cream Dipping Sauce

Serves: 3

Serving size:
   1/3 recipe

4 ounces light cream cheese
2 tablespoons sugar
3/4 teaspoon ground cinnamon
1/4 cup fat-free half-and-half or fat-free milk
1/2 teaspoon vanilla
2 6-ounce pears, sliced

1 Combine cream cheese, sugar, and cinnamon in a small mixing bowl. Using an electric mixer on low speed, beat until well blended.

2 Add half-and-half and vanilla and blend until smooth. Serve with pears.

Exchanges
1 1/2 Fat
2 Carbohydrate

Calories 201
   Calories from Fat 78
Total Fat ....9 g
   Saturated Fat ....5 g
Cholesterol ....28 mg
Sodium ....188 mg
Carbohydrate ....27 g
   Dietary Fiber................3 g
   Sugars ....23 g
Protein ....5 g

Serves: 4

Serving size:
   1 bagel half plus
   1/4 cup veggies

Beyond a Bagel

2 small plain bagels (2 ounces each), cut in half
2 ounces reduced-fat cream cheese
1 teaspoon dried oregano leaves
1/2 cup finely chopped tomato
   1 tablespoon plus 1 teaspoon capers, drained
1/2 cup celery sticks
3/4 cup baby carrots

1 Lightly toast bagels in toaster. Spread each half with 1/2 ounce cream cheese.

2 Sprinkle each half with equal amounts of oregano, tomato, and capers. Serve with veggies.

Exchanges
1 1/2 Starch
2 Vegetable
1/2 Fat

Calories....................185
   Calories from Fat......36
Total Fat.......................4 g
   Saturated Fat...............2 g
Cholesterol.................10 mg
Sodium.......................419 mg
Carbohydrate.............32 g
   Dietary Fiber...............5 g
   Sugars...........................8 g
Protein..........................7 g

BREAKFASTS

3
Carb Exchanges

Serves: 6

Serving size:
   1/6 recipe

Morning Shortcakes with Vanilla Blackberries

1 pound frozen unsweetened blackberries, thawed
3 tablespoons sugar
1/2 teaspoon vanilla
1 1/2 teaspoons grated lemon rind, divided
1 cup plus 2 tablespoons reduced-fat biscuit mix
1 cup fat-free artificially sweetened vanilla-flavored yogurt, divided

Try it with

2 ounces cooked kielbasa turkey sausage
1/2 small orange

Total meal:
   3 carb exchanges

1 Preheat oven to 425°F.

2 In a medium bowl, combine blackberries, sugar, vanilla, and 1/2 teaspoon lemon rind and set aside.

3 In another medium bowl, combine biscuit mix, 1/2 cup plus 2 tablespoons yogurt, and remaining lemon rind. Mix until just blended.

4 Coat a nonstick baking sheet with cooking spray, add dough in 6 mounds, and bake 8–10 minutes or until lightly golden.

5 To serve, place 1 shortcake in each of 6 shallow soup bowls and top each with equal amounts of the berry mixture and the remaining yogurt.

Exchanges
1 Starch
1 Fruit
1/2 Carbohydrate

Calories.....................174
   Calories from Fat......18
Total Fat........................2 g
   Saturated Fat...............0 g
Cholesterol...................1 mg
Sodium......................302 mg
Carbohydrate............37 g
   Dietary Fiber...............4 g
   Sugars.......................17 g
Protein...........................4 g

Crispy Breakfast Pita Rounds

Serves: 4

Serving size:
  1 pita round

2 6-inch pita breads
2 veggie breakfast patties, cut into 1/4-inch pieces
1/4 medium green bell pepper, finely chopped
1 plum tomato, finely chopped
1/4 cup finely chopped green onion
1/4 teaspoon dried red pepper flakes, optional
1 cup shredded reduced-fat sharp cheddar or
  part-skim mozzarella cheese

1 Preheat oven to 475°F.

2 Using a sharp knife, carefully cut each pita so that the top half comes off the bottom half, forming 4 thin rounds.

3 Place pita rounds on a baking sheet. In the order listed, top each round with equal amounts of all ingredients. Bake 5 minutes or until cheese melts.

Try it with

1 cup diced cantaloupe
1/4 cup blueberries
3/4 cup low-sodium
  vegetable juice

Total meal:
  3 carb exchanges

Exchanges

1 1/2 Starch
1 Lean Meat
1 Fat

Calories 209
  Calories from Fat 70
Total Fat ....8 g
  Saturated Fat ....4 g
Cholesterol ....20 mg
Sodium ....537 mg
Carbohydrate ....20 g
  Dietary Fiber ....2 g
  Sugars ....2 g
Protein ....15 g

Serves: 4

Serving size:
  2 muffin halves

■
Try it with

1 cup diced honeydew
  melon
2 Canadian bacon slices,
  heated

Total meal:
  3 carb exchanges

Exchanges

2 Starch
1 High-Fat Meat
1/2 Fat

Calories 282
  Calories from Fat....110
Total Fat ....12 g
  Saturated Fat ....6 g
Cholesterol ....29 mg
Sodium ....551 mg
Carbohydrate ....29 g
  Dietary Fiber ....2 g
  Sugars ....3 g
Protein ....13 g

Swiss Cheese Melt

2 1/2 tablespoons light mayonnaise
1 1/2 tablespoons Dijon mustard
    1 teaspoon dried tarragon leaves
    4 whole English muffins, halved
  1/2 cup finely chopped green onion
    4 ounces sliced Swiss cheese, torn in small pieces

1 Preheat broiler.

2 In a small bowl, combine mayonnaise, mustard, and tarragon and set aside. Spread 1 1/2 teaspoons of the mayonnaise mixture evenly over each muffin half and place on baking sheet. Top each half with equal amounts of onion and cheese.

3 Broil 3 minutes or until cheese melts and begins to brown on edges.

Spinach-Onion Frittata

Serves: 6

Serving size:
  1/6 recipe

1 10-ounce package frozen chopped spinach,
  thawed and squeezed dry
1/2 cup low-fat small curd cottage cheese
1 cup egg substitute
1 teaspoon dried oregano leaves
1/2 teaspoon salt
1/8 teaspoon cayenne
1 14-ounce can artichoke hearts, drained and
  coarsely chopped
3 medium yellow onions, chopped
1 cup shredded reduced-fat sharp cheddar cheese

1 Preheat broiler.

2 In a medium mixing bowl, combine spinach,
cottage cheese, egg substitute, oregano, salt, and
cayenne. Blend well, stir in artichokes, and set aside.

3 Place a 12-inch nonstick skillet over medium
heat until hot. Coat skillet with cooking spray
and cook onion 6–8 minutes or until translucent,
stirring frequently.

4 Add spinach mixture and spread evenly over
bottom of skillet. Reduce heat to medium low,
cover tightly, and cook 15 minutes or until almost
set. (The frittata will be very moist at this point
because of all the onion. It will set when the cheese
is added.)

5 Sprinkle cheese evenly over all and broil
1–2 minutes to melt cheese and finish cooking.
Remove from broiler and let stand 5 minutes to
allow flavors to blend. Cut into 6 wedges to serve.
This dish reheats well.

Try it with

1 piece whole wheat toast
1 teaspoon reduced-fat
  margarine
2 tomato slices
1 medium orange

Total meal:
  3 carb exchanges

Exchanges

1 Medium-Fat Meat
2 Vegetable

Calories	134
Calories from Fat	41
Total Fat	5 g
Saturated Fat	2 g
Cholesterol	14 mg
Sodium	654 mg
Carbohydrate	12 g
Dietary Fiber	3 g
Sugars	5 g
Protein	14 g

Serves: 4

Serving size:
  2 muffin halves
  plus spread

English Muffins with Apricot-Ginger Spread

1/4 cup reduced-fat margarine
1/4 cup apricot 100% fruit spread
  1 teaspoon grated gingerroot
  1 teaspoon honey
  4 whole wheat English muffins, halved

1 In a small mixing bowl, combine all ingredients except muffins and stir to blend. The mixture will be lumpy.

2 Toast muffins and spread equal amounts of the mixture on each muffin half. The spread will melt into the muffins.

Try it with

1/2 cup egg substitute, scrambled
3/4 cup diced cantaloupe

Total meal:
  3 carb exchanges

Exchanges

2 Starch
1 Fat
1/2 Carbohydrate

Calories 218
  Calories from Fat 59
Total Fat .... 7 g
  Saturated Fat .... 1 g
Cholesterol .... 0 mg
Sodium .... 318 mg
Carbohydrate .... 37 g
  Dietary Fiber .... 3 g
  Sugars .... 13 g
Protein .... 6 g

The Stacked Scramble

Serves: 4

Serving size:
  1/4 recipe

2 cups egg substitute
1/3 cup fat-free evaporated milk
2 medium tomatoes, seeded and chopped
1/2 medium green bell pepper, finely chopped
1/4 cup chopped cilantro or parsley leaves
1/4 teaspoon salt
1/4 teaspoon black pepper
1/8 teaspoon cayenne pepper, optional
1 cup shredded reduced-fat sharp cheddar cheese

1 Preheat broiler.

2 In a medium mixing bowl, combine egg substitute and milk and stir to blend.

3 Place a 12-inch ovenproof skillet over medium heat until hot. Coat skillet with cooking spray, add eggs, and cook 2 minutes, lifting cooked portion up with a spatula to allow uncooked portion to flow underneath.

4 Remove skillet from heat and sprinkle eggs evenly with remaining ingredients in the order given. Broil 2 minutes or until cheese melts.

Try it with

2 slices whole wheat toast
2 teaspoons reduced-fat margarine
1/2 medium orange

Total meal:
  3 carb exchanges

Exchanges

2 Lean Meat
2 Vegetable

Calories 174
  Calories from Fat 57
Total Fat .... 6 g
  Saturated Fat .... 4 g
Cholesterol .... 20 mg
Sodium .... 647 mg
Carbohydrate .... 9 g
  Dietary Fiber .... 1 g
  Sugars .... 5 g
Protein .... 21 g

Tortillas with Refried Beans and Cheese

4 corn tortillas
1 cup canned fat-free refried beans
1/2 teaspoon ground cumin
1 cup shredded part-skim mozzarella cheese
1 cup egg substitute
1/4 cup fat-free milk
1/4 cup picante sauce
1/4 cup chopped cilantro leaves, optional
1 medium lime, cut in fourths

Try it with

2 slices cooked bacon
1 medium nectarine,
  sliced
1/3 cup raspberries

Total meal:
  3 carb exchanges

1 Preheat oven to 350°F.

2 Place tortillas on a baking sheet and spread beans evenly over each tortilla. Sprinkle with cumin and cheese. Bake 10 minutes or until cheese melts.

3 Meanwhile, in a small bowl, whisk together egg substitute and milk. Place a 12-inch nonstick skillet over medium heat until hot, add eggs, and cook 2 minutes, lifting cooked portion up with a spatula to allow uncooked portion to flow underneath.

4 Place equal amounts of egg on top of tortillas and spoon picante sauce and cilantro on top. Serve with lime wedges.

Exchanges
1 1/2 Starch
2 Lean Meat

Calories 217
  Calories from Fat 47
Total Fat ....5 g
  Saturated Fat ....3 g
Cholesterol ....16 mg
Sodium ....661 mg
Carbohydrate ....24 g
  Dietary Fiber ....4 g
  Sugars ....2 g
Protein ....18 g

Sausage and Green Onion Strata

Serves: 4

Serving size:
  1/4 recipe

  6 ounces 50% less fat pork sausage
  1 cup fat-free milk
3/4 cup egg substitute
  2 teaspoons Dijon mustard
1/2 cup shredded reduced-fat sharp cheddar cheese
1/4 cup finely chopped green onion
1/2 teaspoon dried thyme leaves
1/4 teaspoon dried red pepper flakes
  3 ounces French bread, cubed

1 Preheat oven to 350°F.

2 Place a 10-inch nonstick skillet over medium high heat until hot. Add sausage and cook until browned and crumbled. Remove skillet from heat and drain sausage on paper towels.

3 Coat a 9-inch pie pan with cooking spray. In a medium bowl, combine sausage with remaining ingredients except bread and stir to blend. Add bread and coat lightly with the egg mixture, being sure that all bread pieces are moistened.

4 Pour strata into pie pan and bake, uncovered, 30 minutes or until knife inserted comes out clean.

Try it with

  1 small banana
3/4 cup no-salt-added
      tomato juice, chilled

Total meal:
  3 carb exchanges

Exchanges

1 Starch
2 Medium-Fat Meat

Calories 239
  Calories from Fat....108
Total Fat ....12 g
  Saturated Fat ....4 g
Cholesterol ....40 mg
Sodium ....689 mg
Carbohydrate ....16 g
  Dietary Fiber................1 g
  Sugars...........................4 g
Protein ....20 g

LUNCHES

3
Carb Exchanges

No-Chop Italian Soup

1 14.5-ounce can diced tomatoes with green
   peppers and onion
1 14-ounce can low-fat reduced-sodium chicken
   broth
8 ounces frozen mixed pepper stir-fry
8 ounces sliced mushrooms
1 tablespoon dried basil leaves
1/2 teaspoon sugar
1/8 teaspoon dried red pepper flakes, optional
   9 ounces frozen cooked diced chicken breast meat
1 tablespoon extra virgin olive oil

1 Combine all ingredients except chicken and oil
   in a medium saucepot. Bring to a boil, reduce
heat, cover tightly, and simmer 30 minutes.

2 Add chicken and olive oil and cook 5 minutes
   longer or until heated thoroughly. If time
allows, remove soup from heat and let stand 10
minutes to allow flavors to blend.

Try it with

1 small roll
1 tablespoon reduced-fat
   margarine
4 ounces low-fat vanilla
   yogurt

Total meal:
   3 carb exchanges

Exchanges

3 Very Lean Meat
3 Vegetable
1 Fat

Calories	209
Calories from Fat	54
Total Fat	6 g
Saturated Fat	1 g
Cholesterol	54 mg
Sodium	687 mg
Carbohydrate	14 g
Dietary Fiber	3 g
Sugars	9 g
Protein	24 g

Country Chicken Stew

Serves: 4

Serving size:
  1 1/4 cups

4 ounces sliced mushrooms
8 ounces frozen mixed pepper stir-fry
1 stalk celery, thinly sliced
1 medium yellow squash, diced
1/4 teaspoon dried thyme leaves
1 10 3/4-ounce can 98% fat-free reduced-sodium
   cream of chicken soup
9 ounces frozen cooked diced chicken breast meat
1/2 cup frozen green peas
1/4 teaspoon salt

1 Place a medium saucepot over medium high heat until hot. Coat skillet with cooking spray and add mushrooms, pepper stir-fry, celery, squash, and thyme.

2 Cook 3 minutes and add soup. Bring just to a boil, reduce heat, cover tightly, and simmer 30 minutes, stirring occasionally.

3 Stir in remaining ingredients and cook 5 minutes longer to heat thoroughly.

Try it with

1 cup shredded cabbage
2 tablespoons reduced-fat
  salad dressing
1 slice pumpkin pie
  (1/8 pie)

Total meal:
  3 carb exchanges

Exchanges
3 Very Lean Meat
1 Vegetable
1 Carbohydrate

Calories 208
   Calories from Fat 38
Total Fat ....4 g
   Saturated Fat ....1 g
Cholesterol ....60 mg
Sodium ....529 mg
Carbohydrate ....17 g
   Dietary Fiber ....3 g
   Sugars ....6 g
Protein ....24 g

Easy Mexican Soup

1 boil-in-bag rice packet
2 14-ounce cans low-fat reduced-sodium chicken
   broth
8 ounces frozen cooked cubed chicken breast meat
1 10.5-ounce can tomatoes with green chilies,
   Mexican-style, drained
1/4 cup chopped cilantro leaves
1/2 medium avocado, diced
1–2 medium limes, cut in wedges

1 In a medium saucepot, cook rice according to directions on package, omitting any salt or fats. When cooked, place rice in a separate bowl and set aside.

2 Discard water for rice and add chicken broth to saucepot. Bring to a boil, add frozen chicken, and return just to a boil. Reduce heat and simmer 2 minutes to heat chicken thoroughly.

3 To serve, place 1/2 cup rice in the bottom of 4 individual shallow soup bowls, spoon 3/4 cup chicken around the mound of rice, top rice with 2 tablespoons tomatoes and 1 tablespoon cilantro, and sprinkle 2 tablespoons avocado around sides. Squeeze lime over all.

Try it with

3 baked tortilla chips
1/2 cup pineapple chunks

Total meal:
   3 carb exchanges

Exchanges

1 1/2 Starch
2 Very Lean Meat
1 Fat

Calories 234
   Calories from Fat 50
Total Fat .... 6 g
   Saturated Fat .... 1 g
Cholesterol .... 48 mg
Sodium .... 350 mg
Carbohydrate .... 25 g
   Dietary Fiber .... 2 g
   Sugars .... 1 g
Protein .... 21 g

Crunchy Spring Greens with Dates and Blue Cheese

Serves: 4

Serving size:
    1/4 recipe

    1 ounce walnut or pecan pieces
1/2 of a .3-ounce package dried Oriental noodle
    soup mix (discard seasoning packet)
    8 cups mixed spring greens
1/2 cup thinly sliced red onion
    9 ounces frozen cooked diced chicken breast
    meat, thawed
1/2 cup chopped dates
1/4 cup balsamic vinegar
    3 tablespoons sugar
1/4 teaspoon salt
1 1/2 ounces crumbled blue cheese

1 Place a 12-inch nonstick skillet over medium high heat until hot. Add nuts and noodle soup mix and cook 2–3 minutes or until beginning to brown.

2 Remove from heat and set aside on separate plate.

3 On 4 individual dinner plates, arrange equal amounts of greens, onion, chicken, dates, and toasted nut mixture.

4 In a small jar, combine vinegar, sugar, and salt. Seal lid tightly and shake vigorously until well blended.

5 Pour dressing evenly over each salad. Top with blue cheese.

Try it with

2 crisp breadsticks
    (4 × 1/2 inches long)
Iced mixed berry green tea

Total meal:
    3 carb exchanges

Exchanges

1 Starch
2 Lean Meat
1 Vegetable
1 1/2 Fruit
1 Fat

Calories	360
Calories from Fat	106
Total Fat	12 g
Saturated Fat	3 g
Cholesterol	62 mg
Sodium	383 mg
Carbohydrate	40 g
Dietary Fiber	3 g
Sugars	28 g
Protein	26 g

Try it with

17 seedless grapes

Total meal:
   3 carb exchanges

Exchanges

1 1/2 Starch
1 Vegetable
1 1/2 Fat

Calories 196
   Calories from Fat 72
Total Fat ....8 g
   Saturated Fat ....2 g
Cholesterol ....10 mg
Sodium ....537 mg
Carbohydrate ....25 g
   Dietary Fiber ....3 g
   Sugars ....4 g
Protein ....8 g

South of the Border BLT Wrap

   8 reduced-sodium bacon slices
1/2 cup fat-free sour cream
1/2 teaspoon lime juice
6–8 drops hot pepper sauce
1/4 teaspoon salt
1/4 teaspoon black pepper
   4 6-inch fat-free flour tortillas
   4 romaine lettuce leaves, rinsed and patted dry
   1 large tomato, cut in 8 slices
1/2 medium avocado, peeled and diced
   1 medium lime, cut in fourths, optional

1 Place paper towels on a microwave-safe plate and put 4 slices bacon in a single layer on top. Cover with paper towels and cook 3 minutes on HIGH setting.

2 Repeat process with remaining bacon slices (working in two batches cooks the bacon more evenly.)

3 Meanwhile, in a small mixing bowl, combine sour cream, lime juice, hot sauce, and salt and stir until well blended. Set aside.

4 Place tortillas on a work surface. On each tortilla, place 1 lettuce leaf, 2 bacon slices, 2 tomato slices, 2 tablespoons sour cream, and 1/4 of the avocado. Fold or roll tortillas, secure with wooden toothpicks, and cut in half. Serve with lime wedges.

Open-Faced Hot Chicken and Swiss Melt

Serves: 4

Serving size:
 1 open-faced sandwich

4 ounces French bread, sliced diagonally in 4 pieces
4 4-ounce boneless skinless chicken breast halves,
  rinsed and patted dry
1/2 cup finely chopped green onion
2 ounces Swiss cheese
2 tablespoons plus 2 teaspoons light mayonnaise
2 tablespoons Dijon mustard
1 teaspoon dried oregano leaves
2 cups mixed spring greens

1 Lightly toast bread.

2 Place a 12-inch nonstick skillet over medium high heat until hot. Coat skillet with cooking spray, add chicken, and cook 4 minutes. Turn and cook 4 more minutes or until chicken is no longer pink in center.

3 Remove chicken from heat, sprinkle with onion, and top with cheese. Cover to allow cheese to melt.

4 In a small bowl, combine mayonnaise, mustard, and oregano and spread on toasted bread. Arrange greens on 4 bread pieces and top each with 1 piece chicken.

Try it with

14 fat-free potato chips
 1 small apple

Total meal:
 3 carb exchanges

Exchanges

1 Starch
4 Lean Meat

Calories 305
  Calories from Fat 94
Total Fat ....10 g
  Saturated Fat ....4 g
Cholesterol ....85 mg
Sodium ....533 mg
Carbohydrate.............18 g
  Dietary Fiber...............1 g
  Sugars..........................2 g
Protein.......................33 g

Serves: 5

Serving size:
 1 1/2 cups

Try it with

1 cup cucumber slices
2 tablespoons reduced-fat
  salad dressing
Sugar-free lemonade

Total meal:
  3 carb exchanges

Exchanges

2 Starch
1 Medium-Fat Meat
1 Vegetable
1 Fat

Calories	298
Calories from Fat	92
Total Fat	10 g
Saturated Fat	3 g
Cholesterol	13 mg
Sodium	741 mg
Carbohydrate	38 g
Dietary Fiber	3 g
Sugars	4 g
Protein	14 g

Tomato-Mozzarella Penne Salad with Capers

8 ounces uncooked dry penne pasta
2 cups cherry tomatoes, preferably sweet grape
  variety, halved
4 ounces part-skim mozzarella cheese, cut in
  1/4-inch cubes
1/2 cup chopped parsley leaves
1/3 cup capers, drained
  2 tablespoons extra virgin olive oil
  2 teaspoons dried basil leaves
  1 garlic clove, minced
3/4 teaspoon salt
1/4 teaspoon dried red pepper flakes, optional
  1 medium lemon

1 Cook pasta according to directions on package, omitting any salt or fats.

2 Meanwhile, in a large mixing bowl, combine remaining ingredients except lemon. Grate 1/2 teaspoon lemon rind and add to the tomato mixture. Squeeze the juice of the lemon over all and set aside.

3 Drain pasta in a colander and rinse under cold water until completely cooled. Drain completely and add to tomato mixture. Toss well and serve.

DINNERS

3
Carb Exchanges

Serving size:
  2 drumsticks plus
  1/3 cup vegetables

Try it with

3/4 cup cooked orzo pasta
1/2 cup steamed
    asparagus pieces
  2 tomato slices

Total meal:
  3 carb exchanges

Exchanges

2 Lean Meat
2 Vegetable

Calories	150
Calories from Fat	34
Total Fat	4 g
Saturated Fat	1 g
Cholesterol	55 mg
Sodium	494 mg
Carbohydrate	11 g
Dietary Fiber	2 g
Sugars	6 g
Protein	18 g

Greek Lemon Drumsticks with Peppers

  8 chicken drumsticks, skinned, rinsed, and
    patted dry
  1 medium green bell pepper, thinly sliced
  2 medium yellow onions, thinly sliced
  2 medium lemons
1 1/2 teaspoons dried oregano leaves
  1/4 teaspoon garlic powder
  3/4 teaspoon salt, divided
  1/8 teaspoon black pepper
    Paprika to taste

1 Preheat oven to 350°F.

2 In a 9 × 13-inch baking pan, combine chicken, bell pepper, and onion. Squeeze the juice of one lemon evenly over all. Grate 1 teaspoon lemon rind and sprinkle over chicken along with oregano, garlic powder, 1/2 teaspoon salt, pepper, and paprika.

3 Lightly coat all with cooking spray and bake, uncovered, for 30 minutes. Turn pieces and cook 30–40 minutes longer or until chicken is no longer pink in center.

4 When chicken is done, place on serving platter. Add remaining 1/4 teaspoon salt and juice of the remaining lemon to vegetables and pan drippings.

5 Stir to blend, scraping bottom and sides of pan. Spoon mixture over chicken.

Smothered Mexican Chicken

Serves: 4

Serving size:
  1 breast half plus
  3/4 cup rice

1 1/2 cups water
  3/4 cup uncooked brown or white rice
    4 4-ounce boneless skinless chicken breast halves,
      rinsed and patted dry
    1 tablespoon lime juice
  3/4 teaspoon ground cumin
  1/4 teaspoon salt
    1 4-ounce can chopped green chilies
    1 small tomato, seeded and diced
  1/4 cup chopped cilantro leaves
    1 cup shredded part-skim mozzarella cheese or
      reduced-fat sharp cheddar cheese

Try it with

1/2 cup cooked yellow
  squash
  1 small orange

Total meal:
  3 carb exchanges

1 Preheat oven to 400°F.

2 In a small saucepan, bring water to a boil and add rice. Reduce heat, cover tightly, and simmer 25–30 minutes or until water is absorbed.

3 Meanwhile, place chicken breasts in a 9 × 13-inch baking dish. Sprinkle evenly with lime juice, cumin, and salt. Spoon green chilies evenly over all. Top with tomato, cilantro, and cheese.

4 Bake, uncovered, 22–25 minutes or until chicken is no longer pink in center. Place rice on serving platter and top with chicken and accumulated juices.

Exchanges
2 Starch
4 Very Lean Meat
1 Fat

Calories 347
  Calories from Fat 77
Total Fat .... 9 g
  Saturated Fat .... 4 g
Cholesterol .... 84 mg
Sodium .... 469 mg
Carbohydrate .... 30 g
  Dietary Fiber .... 2 g
  Sugars .... 1 g
Protein .... 35 g

Pizza Chicken Rolls

Serves: 4

Serving size:
   1 pizza roll plus
   1/2 cup pasta

Try it with

1 small whole-grain roll
1 cup spinach leaves
1/2 ounce crumbled feta
   cheese
2 tablespoons reduced-
   fat salad dressing

Total meal:
   3 carb exchanges

Exchanges

1 1/2 Starch
4 Lean Meat

Calories	357
Calories from Fat	90
Total Fat	10 g
Saturated Fat	5 g
Cholesterol	95 mg
Sodium	680 mg
Carbohydrate	25 g
Dietary Fiber	1 g
Sugars	3 g
Protein	38 g

4 ounces uncooked dry spaghetti
4 4-ounce boneless skinless chicken breast halves,
   rinsed, patted dry, and flattened to 1/4-inch thick
1 1/2 teaspoons dried basil leaves, divided
   16 turkey pepperoni slices
   4 mozzarella string cheese sticks
1/2 cup bottled or canned pizza sauce
1/2 teaspoon red pepper flakes
   4 teaspoons grated Parmesan cheese

1 Preheat oven to 400°F.

2 Cook pasta according to directions on package, omitting any salt or fats.

3 Meanwhile, coat a nonstick baking sheet with cooking spray and arrange chicken on the sheet in a single layer. Sprinkle chicken evenly with 1 teaspoon basil.

4 Line 4 pepperoni slices down the center of each chicken piece, overlapping slightly. Place a stick of cheese on top of the pepperoni, fold over sides of chicken, and place seam side down.

5 Top each roll with 2 tablespoons pizza sauce. Sprinkle evenly with remaining 1/2 teaspoon basil and red pepper flakes.

6 Bake 22 minutes or until chicken is no longer pink in center and cheese is beginning to melt. Sprinkle each piece with 1 teaspoon Parmesan cheese. Serve on cooked spaghetti.

Seared Sirloin with Sweet Balsamic Sauce

Serves: 4

Serving size:
  1/4 recipe

1 pound boneless sirloin steak, trimmed of fat,
  about 1 inch thick
1/4 cup water
  1 tablespoon light soy sauce
  1 tablespoon Worcestershire sauce
  1 tablespoon balsamic vinegar
  1 tablespoon sugar

1 Place a 12-inch nonstick skillet over medium
  high heat until hot. Add beef and cook 4 minutes. Turn and cook 4 minutes longer or until beef is done to your liking.

2 Meanwhile, in a small bowl, combine remaining sauce ingredients. Stir to blend and set aside.

3 When beef is done, place on cutting board and let stand. Add sauce mixture to pan residue in skillet. Bring to a boil over medium high heat and cook 1–2 minutes, scraping bottom and sides of skillet.

4 Thinly slice beef and spoon sauce over all.

Try it with

2/3 cup cooked brown or
  white rice
1/2 cup steamed snow
  peas
1/2 cup cucumber slices
  2 tablespoons chopped
  green onion
  1 tablespoon reduced-
  fat salad dressing

Total meal:
  3 carb exchanges

Exchanges

3 Lean Meat
1/2 Carbohydrate

Calories 174
  Calories from Fat 51
Total Fat .... 6 g
  Saturated Fat .... 2 g
Cholesterol .... 69 mg
Sodium .... 266 mg
Carbohydrate .... 5 g
  Dietary Fiber .... 0 g
  Sugars .... 5 g
Protein .... 24 g

Serves: 4

Serving size:
  1 patty

Try it with

1/2 cup prepared
    refrigerated mashed
    potatoes
  1 small sourdough roll
  1 cup steamed broccoli
    seasoned with butter
    spray and fresh lemon
    juice

Total meal:
  3 carb exchanges

Exchanges
3 Lean Meat

Calories	179
Calories from Fat	35
Total Fat	4 g
Saturated Fat	1 g
Cholesterol	64 mg
Sodium	289 mg
Carbohydrate	3 g
Dietary Fiber	1 g
Sugars	1 g
Protein	27 g

Beef Patties with Burgundy Mushrooms

  8 ounces sliced mushrooms
  1 pound 96% extra-lean ground beef, shaped into
    4 even patties
1/2 cup dry red wine
  1 teaspoon beef bouillon granules
1/2 teaspoon dried oregano leaves
1/4 teaspoon black pepper

1 Place a 12-inch nonstick skillet over medium high heat until hot. Coat skillet with cooking spray, add mushrooms, and sauté 5 minutes. Remove mushrooms from skillet and set aside on separate plate.

2 Add beef patties to skillet, reduce heat to medium, and cook 4 minutes. Turn and cook 4 minutes longer or until burgers are done to your liking.

3 Meanwhile, in a small bowl, combine remaining ingredients, add mushrooms and any accumulated juices, and set aside.

4 Place beef patties on a serving platter and cover with a sheet of foil to keep warm.

5 Add mushroom mixture to pan residue, increase heat to high, and bring to a boil. Continue boiling 1 minute or until reduced slightly. Spoon over beef patties.

Crab and Red Pepper Casserole

Serves: 4

Serving size:
1 cup

2 ounces French bread, torn in small pieces
1 medium red bell pepper, chopped
1/2 cup chopped green onion
1/2 cup fat-free half-and-half or evaporated milk
1/3 cup reduced-fat margarine
2 tablespoons Dijon mustard
1/4 teaspoon seafood seasoning
1/4 teaspoon cayenne pepper
1 pound fresh crab meat, picked through
1/4 cup chopped parsley leaves
1 tablespoon grated Parmesan cheese

1 Preheat oven to 350°F.

2 Place bread in food processor and pulse to bread crumb consistency.

3 Place a 12-inch nonstick skillet over medium high heat until hot. Coat skillet with cooking spray, add bell pepper, and cook 5 minutes or until just tender.

4 Remove from heat and stir in green onion, half-and-half, margarine, mustard, seasoning, and cayenne. Stir to blend well. Add 3/4 cup bread crumbs, crab, and parsley and stir until just blended.

5 Sprinkle with remaining bread crumbs, coat lightly with cooking spray, and bake 20 minutes or until heated thoroughly and bread crumbs begin to lightly brown.

6 Remove from oven and sprinkle with Parmesan cheese.

Try it with

1/2 cup steamed carrots seasoned with butter spray
1/2 cup quartered cherry tomatoes
1/4 cup quartered artichoke hearts
1 tablespoon reduced-fat salad dressing
1 ounce French bread

Total meal:
3 carb exchanges

Exchanges

3 Lean Meat
1 Carbohydrate

Calories 245
Calories from Fat 89
Total Fat .... 10 g
Saturated Fat .... 2 g
Cholesterol .... 72 mg
Sodium .... 818 mg
Carbohydrate .... 15 g
Dietary Fiber .... 2 g
Sugars .... 4 g
Protein .... 24 g

Baked Grouper with Tomato-Caper Salsa

Try it with

1/3 cup cooked orzo or
    angel hair pasta
  1 ounce Italian bread
  1 teaspoon reduced-fat
    margarine
  1 cup mixed greens
  2 tablespoons reduced-
    fat salad dressing
3/4 cup strawberries

Total meal:
  3 carb exchanges

  4 4-ounce grouper filets, rinsed and patted dry
    Paprika to taste
1/4 teaspoon salt
1/2 teaspoon black pepper
  5 ounces sweet grape cherry tomatoes, quartered
 12 kalamata olives, pitted and coarsely chopped
1/4 cup capers, drained
1/4 cup chopped parsley
1/2 medium garlic clove, minced
  1 medium lemon, cut in fourths

1 Preheat oven to 400°F.

2 Coat a nonstick baking sheet with cooking spray, arrange filets on baking sheet, and sprinkle paprika, salt, and pepper evenly over all. Bake 10–12 minutes or until opaque in center.

3 Meanwhile, in a mixing bowl, combine tomatoes, olives, capers, parsley, and garlic and set aside.

4 When fish is cooked, place on 4 dinner plates, squeeze lemon fourth over each serving, and top with tomato mixture.

Exchanges

3 Very Lean Meat
1 Vegetable

Calories 130
  Calories from Fat 22
Total Fat .... 2 g
  Saturated Fat .... 0 g
Cholesterol .... 42 mg
Sodium .... 538 mg
Carbohydrate .... 4 g
  Dietary Fiber .... 1 g
  Sugars .... 1 g
Protein .... 23 g

White Wine and Tarragon Scallops

Serves: 4

Serving size:
  1/4 recipe

3/4 teaspoon dried tarragon leaves
1/4 teaspoon paprika
1/4–1/2 teaspoon black pepper
1 1/2 pounds scallops, rinsed and patted dry
1 tablespoon extra virgin olive oil
1 tablespoon margarine
1/2 cup dry white wine
2 tablespoons lemon juice
1/4 teaspoon salt
2 tablespoons chopped parsley leaves or finely chopped green onion

1 In a small bowl, combine tarragon, paprika, and pepper. Mix well.

2 Sprinkle scallops evenly with the tarragon mixture.

3 Place a 12-inch nonstick skillet over medium high heat until hot. Add oil and margarine. When margarine has melted, add half the scallops and cook 3 minutes. Turn and cook 2 minutes longer or until scallops are opaque in center, using 2 utensils to turn scallops easily.

4 Remove scallops from skillet and set aside on serving platter. Cover to keep warm and repeat with remaining scallops.

5 Add wine to pan residue, increase heat to high, and boil 45 seconds, scraping bottom and sides of pan. Remove pan from heat, add lemon juice and salt to wine sauce, and spoon over scallops. Sprinkle scallops with parsley and serve.

Try it with

1/3 cup cooked angel hair pasta
1 cup steamed asparagus pieces
1 ounce hard roll seasoned with butter spray
1 tomato slice

Total meal:
  3 carb exchanges

Exchanges

4 Very Lean Meat
1 Fat
1/2 Carbohydrate

Calories	225
Calories from Fat	68
Total Fat	8 g
Saturated Fat	1 g
Cholesterol	56 mg
Sodium	456 mg
Carbohydrate	5 g
Dietary Fiber	0 g
Sugars	0 g
Protein	29 g

Calories	317
Calories from Fat	129
Total Fat	14 g
Saturated Fat	5 g
Cholesterol	47 mg
Sodium	748 mg
Carbohydrate	34 g
Dietary Fiber	2 g
Sugars	6 g
Protein	16 g

Sausage and Hash Brown Casserole

6 ounces 50% less fat breakfast pork sausage
1 pound frozen country-style hash brown potatoes
1 medium yellow onion, finely chopped
1 10 3/4-ounce can 98% fat-free cream of
   chicken soup
1/2 cup fat-free half-and-half or evaporated milk
1/2 cup shredded reduced-fat sharp cheddar cheese
1/4 teaspoon black pepper
   Paprika
2 tablespoons chopped parsley leaves

1 Preheat oven to 350°F.

2 Place a 12-inch ovenproof skillet over medium high heat until hot. Cook sausage 2–3 minutes or until browned and crumbled. Drain sausage on paper towels.

3 Add potatoes, onion, soup, milk, cheese, and black pepper to skillet. Sprinkle sausage and paprika evenly over all.

4 Cover tightly and bake 30 minutes or until cheese melts. Remove from oven, sprinkle with parsley, and let stand 5 minutes to allow flavors to blend.

Garlic-Roasted Pork with Tarragon Sauce

Serves: 4

Serving size:
  1/4 recipe

1 pound pork tenderloin
2 garlic cloves, peeled and halved
1/2 teaspoon salt, divided
1/4 teaspoon black pepper
  Paprika
1/2 cup plain fat-free yogurt
1 tablespoon Dijon mustard
1 1/2 teaspoons dried tarragon leaves
2 teaspoons extra virgin olive oil

1 Preheat oven to 425°F.

2 Place pork on a baking sheet. Cut four 1/2-inch slits in pork and place a garlic half in each slit. Sprinkle evenly with 1/4 teaspoon of the salt, pepper, and paprika.

3 Bake 22–24 minutes or until just barely pink in center. When pork is cooked, place on cutting board and let stand 3 minutes before thinly slicing on the diagonal.

4 Just before pork is done, combine remaining ingredients except oil in a small saucepan. Cook 2–3 minutes over medium heat or until just heated through. Do not bring mixture to a boil.

5 Remove from heat, stir in oil, and serve alongside pork for dipping.

Try it with

1 cup mashed sweet
  potato
2 teaspoons reduced-fat
  margarine
1 cup spinach leaves
1/4 cup sliced cucumbers
2 tablespoons reduced-
  fat salad dressing

Total meal:
  3 carb exchanges

Exchanges
3 Lean Meat

Calories 181
  Calories from Fat 59
Total Fat ....7 g
  Saturated Fat ....2 g
Cholesterol ....65 mg
Sodium ....455 mg
Carbohydrate ....4 g
  Dietary Fiber ....0 g
  Sugars ....3 g
Protein ....26 g

Twice-Baked
Stuffed Portabellos

1 medium yellow onion, thinly sliced
1 medium red bell pepper, thinly sliced
4 portabello mushroom caps, wiped clean with
   damp cloth
1/4 teaspoon salt
1/4 teaspoon black pepper
2 cups prepared refrigerated mashed potatoes
2 tablespoons red wine vinegar
3 ounces crumbled blue cheese

1 Preheat oven to 425°F.

2 Arrange onion and bell pepper slices in a single layer on a nonstick baking pan. Liberally coat with cooking spray.

3 Coat both sides of mushrooms with cooking spray and place on top of veggie slices, gill side up. Sprinkle evenly with salt and pepper.

4 Bake 15 minutes or until mushrooms are tender when pierced with a fork and onion slices are beginning to brown lightly.

5 Meanwhile, prepare potatoes according to directions on package, omitting any salt or fats. When vegetables are cooked, remove from oven. Push onion and pepper slices to one side of the baking pan.

6 Spoon 1 1/2 teaspoons vinegar evenly over each mushroom. Sprinkle 3 tablespoons cheese evenly over each mushroom. Spoon 1/2 cup mashed potatoes on top and spoon equal amounts of onion and pepper slices over potatoes.

7 Bake 5–7 minutes to heat thoroughly and melt cheese slightly.

Cheddary Vegetables
au Gratin

Serves: 4

Serving size:
  1/4 recipe

1 1/4 pounds russet potatoes, peeled and thinly sliced
   1 medium yellow onion, chopped
   1 medium yellow squash, sliced
  1/2 medium green bell pepper, chopped
  1/2 medium carrot, grated
   1 tablespoon flour
  1/2 teaspoon dried thyme leaves
  1/2 teaspoon salt, divided
  1/4 teaspoon black pepper, divided
   2 tablespoons reduced-fat margarine
   2 ounces French bread, torn in small pieces
   1 cup shredded reduced-fat sharp cheddar cheese

1 Preheat oven to 400°F.

2 Coat a 9-inch deep-dish pie pan with cooking spray. Layer half the potatoes and onion on the bottom of the pie pan. Top with all the squash, bell pepper, and carrots.

3 Sprinkle evenly with flour and thyme and add 1/4 teaspoon salt and 1/8 teaspoon black pepper. Top with remaining potatoes and onion.

4 Dot evenly with margarine and sprinkle with remaining salt and pepper. Cover with foil and bake 30 minutes or until potatoes are tender-crisp.

5 Meanwhile, place bread in food processor and pulse to bread crumb consistency.

6 Remove foil, top dish with cheese and bread crumbs, and bake 15 minutes longer or until potatoes are tender. Remove from oven and let stand 10 minutes to absorb liquid and allow flavors to blend.

Try it with
  1/2 cup steamed green
    beans
1 1/2 teaspoons reduced-
    fat margarine
   2 tomato slices

Total meal:
  3 carb exchanges

Exchanges

2 Starch
1 Medium-Fat Meat
2 Vegetable
1/2 Fat

Calories 294
  Calories from Fat 81
Total Fat ....9 g
  Saturated Fat ....4 g
Cholesterol ....20 mg
Sodium ....670 mg
Carbohydrate ....43 g
  Dietary Fiber ....6 g
  Sugars ....8 g
Protein ....13 g

BREAKFASTS

4

Carb Exchanges

Sausage and Chunky Maple'd Apples

  2 tablespoons pure maple syrup or honey
    (not pancake syrup)
  1 teaspoon cornstarch
1/2 teaspoon ground cinnamon
1/4 teaspoon ground allspice
1/4 cup water
  1 pound Gala apples, cut in 1-inch chunks
  1 tablespoon reduced-fat margarine
1/2 teaspoon vanilla extract
  4 3-ounce chicken sausage patties with apples

1 In a small bowl, combine syrup, cornstarch, cinnamon, and allspice. Stir until cornstarch is dissolved and set aside.

2 In a medium saucepan, bring water to a boil over high heat. Add apples and return to a boil. Reduce heat, cover tightly, and simmer 3–4 minutes or until apples are just tender crisp.

3 Increase heat to high, stir in syrup mixture, and bring to a boil. Continue boiling 20–30 seconds or until slightly thickened. Remove from heat, stir in margarine and vanilla, cover, and let stand 5 minutes to absorb flavors.

4 Meanwhile, place a 12-inch nonstick skillet over medium heat until hot. Coat skillet with cooking spray and cook sausage 5–7 minutes or until thoroughly heated and beginning to richly brown, turning occasionally. Serve with apples.

Breakfast Sandwich to Go

4 reduced-sodium bacon slices
8 whole wheat bread slices
4 teaspoons reduced-fat margarine
1 1/2 cups egg substitute
1/3 cup fat-free evaporated milk
1/4 teaspoon black pepper
6–8 drops hot pepper sauce
2 slices reduced-fat American cheese, cut in half diagonally

1 Place a layer of paper towels on a microwave-safe plate. Arrange bacon in a single layer and cover with another layer of paper towels. Cook in microwave 3–4 minutes on HIGH setting or until crisp.

2 Place a 12-inch nonstick skillet over medium heat until hot. Coat skillet with cooking spray and add egg substitute, milk, black pepper, and hot pepper sauce. Cook 2 minutes, lifting cooked portion up with a spatula to allow uncooked portion to flow underneath. Remove from heat, top with cheese slices, cover tightly, and let stand 1 minute to let cheese melt.

3 While cheese is melting, toast bread slices and spread 1/2 teaspoon margarine over each piece of toast. Break bacon slices in half and arrange 2 halves on top of 4 pieces of toast. Place 1/4 egg mixture evenly on bacon and top with another piece of toast.

Try it with

1 small banana
1 cup fat-free milk

Total meal:
  4 carb exchanges

Exchanges

2 Starch
2 Lean Meat

Calories 276
  Calories from Fat 78
Total Fat ....9 g
  Saturated Fat ....3 g
Cholesterol ....10 mg
Sodium ....745 mg
Carbohydrate ....30 g
  Dietary Fiber ....4 g
  Sugars ....5 g
Protein ....20 g

Kielbasa Soft Tacos

8 ounces turkey kielbasa or smoked sausage,
   halved lengthwise, then halved crosswise
   (making 4 long pieces)
1/2 medium green bell pepper, chopped
1/2 medium yellow onion, chopped
   2 cups egg substitute
1/4 cup fat-free milk
1/4 cup chopped parsley leaves
   4 10-inch flour tortillas, warmed

Try it with

1 plum

Total meal:
   4 carb exchanges

1 Place a 12-inch nonstick skillet over medium
   high heat until hot. Coat skillet with cooking
spray, add sausage, and cook 2 minutes or until
browned, turning frequently.

2 Remove from skillet and set aside. Recoat skillet
   with cooking spray and reduce heat to medium.
Add bell pepper and onion and cook 5 minutes or
until onion is translucent.

3 Add egg substitute, milk, and parsley and cook
   2 minutes, lifting up edges with a rubber
spatula to allow eggs to cook evenly. Stir gently.

4 Remove from heat and fill tortillas down the
   center with equal amounts of egg mixture. Top
with sausage and serve.

Exchanges

3 Starch
2 Lean Meat
1 Vegetable
1/2 Fat

Calories 397
   Calories from Fat 100
Total Fat .... 11 g
   Saturated Fat .... 3 g
Cholesterol .... 36 mg
Sodium .... 1116 mg
Carbohydrate .... 50 g
   Dietary Fiber .... 4 g
   Sugars .... 6 g
Protein .... 27 g

Creamy Cheese Grits

Serves: 4

Serving size:
  3/4 cup

2 3/4 cups water
  1/2 cup quick-cooking grits
  1/4 teaspoon salt
    4 slices reduced-fat American cheese
  1/2 cup fat-free half-and-half
  1/8 teaspoon cayenne pepper
      Black pepper to taste

1 In a medium saucepan, bring water to boil over high heat. Stir in grits and salt. Reduce heat, cover tightly, and simmer 5 minutes or until most of the liquid has been absorbed.

2 Remove from heat and stir in remaining ingredients except black pepper. Cover and let stand 2–3 minutes to thicken slightly and allow flavors to blend. Sprinkle lightly with black pepper and serve.

Try it with
    1 hard-boiled egg
    2 ounces onion bagel
      (1/2 large), lightly
      toasted
    1 tablespoon
      margarine
  1 1/4 cups strawberries

Total meal:
  4 carb exchanges

Exchanges

1 Starch
1 Lean Meat

Calories 136
  Calories from Fat 33
Total Fat .... 4 g
  Saturated Fat .... 2 g
Cholesterol .... 12 mg
Sodium .... 469 mg
Carbohydrate .... 18 g
  Dietary Fiber .... 1 g
  Sugars .... 3 g
Protein .... 6 g

Serving size:
  2 waffles plus
  1/2 cup berries

Pop-Up Waffles with Sweet and Saucy Berries

3/4 cup fresh or frozen unsweetened blueberries
1 1/2 cups whole strawberries, quartered
1/2 teaspoon ground cinnamon
1/8 teaspoon ground cloves
  2 tablespoons dark brown sugar, packed
1/4 teaspoon almond extract
  8 frozen waffles

1 If using frozen blueberries, place in a colander and run under cold water 10–15 seconds to quickly thaw, but still keep firm. Drain on paper towels and set aside.

2 Place all ingredients except waffles in a medium mixing bowl and mix gently. Let stand 10 minutes to allow flavors to blend.

3 Toast waffles and top with berry mixture.

Try it with

2 veggie breakfast patties
1/3 cup low-fat vanilla yogurt

Total meal:
  4 carb exchanges

Exchanges

2 Starch
1 Fruit
1 Fat

Calories 257
  Calories from Fat 66
Total Fat .... 7 g
  Saturated Fat .... 2 g
Cholesterol .... 20 mg
Sodium .... 405 mg
Carbohydrate .... 44 g
  Dietary Fiber .... 4 g
  Sugars .... 16 g
Protein .... 5 g

Blueberry-Orange Muffins

Serves: 12

Serving size:
  1 muffin

1 1-pound box low-fat blueberry muffin mix
2/3 cup water
1/4 cup egg substitute
1 2.5-ounce jar puréed pears (baby food)
1 tablespoon grated orange zest
3/4 teaspoon ground cinnamon
6 ounces reduced-fat cream cheese

1 Preheat oven to 400°F.

2 Coat a nonstick 12-muffin tin with cooking spray.

3 In a medium mixing bowl, combine all ingredients and stir until just blended. Do not over-mix.

4 Pour batter in muffin cups and bake 14 minutes or until a wooden toothpick inserted comes out clean. Carefully remove muffins from tin and cool on wire rack.

Try it with

2 slices cooked bacon
1 medium banana
1 cup fat-free milk

Total meal:
  4 carb exchanges

Exchanges
2 Carbohydrate

Calories 151
  Calories from Fat 27
Total Fat .... 3 g
  Saturated Fat .... 2 g
Cholesterol .... 10 mg
Sodium .... 259 mg
Carbohydrate .... 27 g
  Dietary Fiber .... 2 g
  Sugars .... 15 g
Protein .... 4 g

Try it with

2 ounces cooked turkey
   sausage
1 medium banana

Total meal:
   4 carb exchanges

___

Exchanges

2 Starch
1/2 Fat
1 Carbohydrate

___

Calories 260
   Calories from Fat 49
Total Fat ....5 g
   Saturated Fat ....1 g
Cholesterol ....1 mg
Sodium ....488 mg
Carbohydrate ....43 g
   Dietary Fiber ....1 g
   Sugars ....14 g
Protein ....10 g

Easy Oven French Toast with Spice Sugar

1/2 cup egg substitute
1/2 cup fat-free milk
   1 teaspoon vanilla or 1/2 teaspoon vanilla, butter,
     and nut flavoring
   8 (1-ounce) diagonally cut slices of French bread
     (about 1 inch thick)
1/4 cup sugar
1/2 teaspoon ground cinnamon
1/4 cup reduced-fat margarine

1 Preheat oven to 450°F.

2 Coat a nonstick baking sheet with cooking spray and set aside. In a shallow dish, such as a pie pan, combine egg substitute, milk, and extract. Stir to blend.

3 Lightly dip both sides of the bread slices into egg mixture. Place bread slices on a baking sheet. Bake 15 minutes or until golden brown.

4 Meanwhile, in a small bowl, combine the sugar and cinnamon and set aside.

5 Place 2 bread slices on each of 4 individual dinner plates, top each slice with 1 1/2 teaspoons reduced-fat margarine, and sprinkle with 1 1/2 teaspoons of the sugar mixture.

LUNCHES
4
Carb Exchanges

Tuna Curry Salad with Pineapple

2 6-ounce cans tuna packed in water, drained
1/4 cup plus 2 tablespoons light mayonnaise
3 tablespoons fat-free milk
1 tablespoon plus 1 teaspoon sugar
3/4 teaspoon curry powder
1 cup finely chopped celery
4 cups mixed spring greens
2 cups pineapple chunks

1 In a medium mixing bowl, combine tuna, mayonnaise, milk, sugar, and curry. Stir until well blended, then stir in celery.

2 Arrange 1 cup greens on each of 4 dinner plates, spoon equal amounts of the tuna mixture in the center of each plate, and arrange pineapple chunks around the tuna.

Try it with

10 reduced-fat Triscuit-
  style crackers
1 cup baby carrots

Total meal:
  4 carb exchanges

Exchanges

3 Lean Meat
1 Fruit

Calories 236
  Calories from Fat 77
Total Fat .... 9 g
  Saturated Fat .... 1 g
Cholesterol .... 29 mg
Sodium .... 481 mg
Carbohydrate .... 19 g
  Dietary Fiber .... 2 g
  Sugars .... 15 g
Protein .... 21 g

Hot Dog Sizzlers with Crispy French Fries

Serves: 4

Serving size:
  1 sizzler with fries

1 pound russet potatoes, scrubbed
1 tablespoon extra virgin olive oil
1/2 teaspoon paprika
1/2 teaspoon dried dill weed, optional
1/8 teaspoon garlic powder
1/8 teaspoon black pepper
  4 hot dog buns
  4 3-ounce reduced-fat hot dogs
1/4 teaspoon salt
  4 teaspoons honey mustard

Try it with

1/2 cup celery sticks
1/2 cup baby carrots

Total meal:
  4 carb exchanges

1 Preheat oven to 475°F.

2 Cut potatoes lengthwise in 1/2-inch slices, then cut each slice in 1/2-inch strips. (To prevent potatoes from wobbling while slicing, slice the end off of one side, then turn the cut side down on the cutting board and continue slicing.)

3 Place fries in a medium bowl, drizzle oil over them, and sprinkle evenly with paprika, dill weed, garlic powder, and black pepper. Toss gently to coat evenly.

4 Arrange fries in a single layer on a nonstick baking sheet and bake on lower oven rack 8 minutes. Flip fries, using 2 utensils to turn easily, and place buns on upper oven rack. Cook 4 more minutes or until fries are tender and buns are warm.

5 Meanwhile, place a 12-inch nonstick skillet over medium heat until hot. Coat skillet with cooking spray, add hot dogs, and cook 5–7 minutes or until hot dogs are golden brown, turning frequently.

6 When fries are done, remove pan from oven, sprinkle fries evenly with salt, and shake pan to coat. Place hot dogs in warm buns, top with honey mustard, and serve with fries.

Exchanges

3 Starch
2 Lean Meat
1 Fat

Calories	386
Calories from Fat	117
Total Fat	13 g
Saturated Fat	3 g
Cholesterol	56 mg
Sodium	921 mg
Carbohydrate	45 g
Dietary Fiber	4 g
Sugars	7 g
Protein	22 g

Mozzarella and Tomato Flatbreads

Try it with

1 cup mixed greens
2 tablespoons reduced-
  fat salad dressing
1/2 cup frozen fat-free
  yogurt

Total meal:
  4 carb exchanges

  4 6-inch whole wheat or white pita rounds
  2 teaspoons bottled minced garlic
  1 cup shredded part-skim mozzarella cheese
  6 ounces plum tomatoes, sliced, or sweet grape
    cherry tomatoes, quartered
1/4 teaspoon salt
  2 ounces thinly sliced yellow onion
1/2 medium green bell pepper, cut in thin slivers
  1 tablespoon dried basil leaves
1/4 teaspoon dried pepper flakes, optional
 12 kalamata olives, pitted and coarsely chopped

1 Preheat oven to 475°F.

2 Place pita rounds on a baking sheet and spread
  1/2 teaspoon garlic evenly over each round.

3 Sprinkle each round equally with remaining
  ingredients in the order given. Spray lightly
with cooking spray.

4 Bake 7–10 minutes or until cheese has melted
  and is beginning to lightly brown on edges.

Exchanges

2 Starch
1 Medium-Fat Meat
1 Vegetable

Calories 245
  Calories from Fat 64
Total Fat .... 7 g
  Saturated Fat .... 3 g
Cholesterol .... 16 mg
Sodium .... 496 mg
Carbohydrate .... 36 g
  Dietary Fiber .... 4 g
  Sugars .... 5 g
Protein .... 13 g

Smoked Turkey Sausage and Peppers on Toasted Pumpernickel

8 ounces smoked turkey sausage
1 medium green bell pepper, thinly sliced
2 medium yellow onions, thinly sliced
3 tablespoons light mayonnaise
1 teaspoon prepared mustard
2 teaspoons honey
1/4 cup water
4 dark pumpernickel bread slices, toasted

1 Cut sausage in half lengthwise, then cut each half in fourths crosswise, forming 8 pieces.

2 Place a 12-inch nonstick skillet over medium high heat until hot. Coat skillet with cooking spray, add sausage, and cook 1 minute. Add bell pepper and onion and cook 4 minutes or until onion is lightly brown, stirring frequently.

3 Meanwhile, in a small bowl, combine mayonnaise, mustard, and honey and stir until well blended. Set aside.

4 Add water to sausage and vegetable mixture and cook 1 minute or until most of the liquid has evaporated, mixing in sausage drippings from the pan bottom as you stir.

5 Remove from heat, spread 1 tablespoon of the mayonnaise mixture evenly over each bread slice, and top with sausage and pepper mixture.

Serves: 4

Serving size:
1/4 recipe

Try it with

1/3 cup baked beans
1 cup fat-free milk

Total meal:
4 carb exchanges

Exchanges

1 1/2 Starch
1 Medium-Fat Meat
1 Vegetable
1 Fat

Calories 258
Calories from Fat 99
Total Fat ....11 g
Saturated Fat ....3 g
Cholesterol ....40 mg
Sodium ....864 mg
Carbohydrate ....33 g
Dietary Fiber ....5 g
Sugars ....10 g
Protein ....12 g

Ham and Dill Potato Salad

        2 cups water
1 1/2 pounds red potatoes, cut into 1/2-inch cubes
    1/3 cup light mayonnaise
      2 tablespoons cider vinegar
      1 tablespoon prepared mustard
      1 tablespoon dried dill weed
    1/4 teaspoon black pepper
      8 ounces extra lean ham, thinly sliced and
        chopped
    3/4 cup finely chopped yellow onion
    1/2 medium green bell pepper, chopped
      1 medium celery stalk, chopped

Try it with

4 whole wheat reduced-
  fat crackers
2 tomato slices
1/2 cup artificially sweetened low-fat pudding

Total meal:
  4 carb exchanges

1 Place a collapsible steamer basket in a 3-quart saucepan. Add 2 cups water, arrange potatoes in basket, and bring to boil over high heat. Cover tightly and steam 7–8 minutes or until potatoes are just tender.

2 Meanwhile, in a medium mixing bowl, combine mayonnaise, vinegar, mustard, dill weed, and black pepper. Stir until well blended. Add remaining ingredients and set aside.

3 Place potatoes in a colander and run under cold water until cooled completely. Shake off excess water. Add potatoes to ham mixture and mix gently, yet thoroughly.

Exchanges

2 Starch
2 Lean Meat
1 Vegetable
1/2 Fat

Calories 315
  Calories from Fat 92
Total Fat .... 10 g
  Saturated Fat .... 2 g
Cholesterol .... 39 mg
Sodium .... 987 mg
Carbohydrate .... 37 g
  Dietary Fiber .... 5 g
  Sugars .... 6 g
Protein .... 19 g

Canadian Bacon and Egg Salad Sandwiches

4 large eggs
3 ounces Canadian bacon, finely chopped
1 cup finely chopped celery
3 tablespoons sweet pickle relish
2 tablespoons light mayonnaise
1/4 cup fat-free milk
1/4 teaspoon black pepper
8 whole wheat bread slices
4 romaine lettuce leaves

1 Place eggs in a small saucepan, add enough cold water to cover eggs, and bring to a boil over high heat. Reduce heat and simmer 10 minutes.

2 Meanwhile, in a medium mixing bowl, combine Canadian bacon, celery, relish, mayonnaise, milk, and pepper.

3 When eggs are done, peel under cold running water. Discard 1 yolk, then chop remaining eggs and stir into bacon mixture.

4 Place a bread slice on each of 4 plates, top with a lettuce leaf, spoon egg salad on lettuce, and top with another bread slice.

Serves: 4

Serving size:
  1 sandwich

Try it with
12 baked tortilla chips
  1 medium peach

Total meal:
  4 carb exchanges

Exchanges
2 Starch
1 Medium-Fat Meat
1 Fat

Calories 282
  Calories from Fat 92
Total Fat ....10 g
  Saturated Fat ....3 g
Cholesterol ....172 mg
Sodium ....806 mg
Carbohydrate ....33 g
  Dietary Fiber ....5 g
  Sugars ....8 g
Protein ....16 g

Serves: 5

Serving size:
   1 cup

Grab-and-Go Taco Chili

12 ounces 96% extra-lean ground beef
1 15.5-ounce can dark kidney beans
8 ounces frozen mixed pepper stir-fry
1 14.5-ounce no-added-salt stewed tomatoes
1 1.25-ounce packet mild taco seasoning mix
1 teaspoon sugar

Try it with

1 ounce low-fat corn
   muffin
1 tangerine
1 cup fat-free milk

Total meal:
   4 carb exchanges

1 Place a saucepot over medium high heat until hot. Coat pot with cooking spray, add beef, and brown 4 minutes, stirring occasionally.

2 Place beans and frozen pepper mixture in a colander and run under cold water to rinse beans and thaw peppers. Shake off excess liquid and add to beef.

3 Add remaining ingredients and bring to a boil. Reduce heat, cover tightly, and simmer 30 minutes.

Exchanges

1 Starch
2 Lean Meat
2 Vegetable

Calories 223
   Calories from Fat 24

Total Fat ....3 g
   Saturated Fat ....1 g
Cholesterol ....38 mg
Sodium ....656 mg
Carbohydrate ....26 g
   Dietary Fiber ....6 g
   Sugars ....7 g
Protein ....22 g

DINNERS

4

Carb Exchanges

Black Bean and Green Chili Skillet Casserole

1 cup water
1/2 cup uncooked brown rice
   3 medium yellow onions, chopped
1/2 teaspoon turmeric, optional
   6 ounces cherry tomatoes, preferably sweet grape
      variety, quartered
   1 15-ounce can black beans, rinsed and drained
   1 4-ounce can chopped green chilies
   1 tablespoon lime juice
3/4 teaspoon ground cumin
1/2 teaspoon salt
   1 cup shredded reduced-fat sharp cheddar cheese

1 In a 10-inch nonstick skillet, bring water to boil over high heat. Add rice, onion, and turmeric and return to a boil. Reduce heat, cover tightly, and simmer 25 minutes or until rice is done.

2 Stir in remaining ingredients except cheese. Remove from heat, top with cheese, cover tightly, and let stand 5 minutes to allow cheese to melt and flavors to blend.

Double-Quick Tomato, White Bean, and Cumin Soup

Serves: 4

Serving size:
 1 1/4 cups

1 14.5-ounce can diced tomatoes with green
   peppers and onion
1 14-ounce can fat-free reduced-sodium
   chicken broth
1 16-ounce can navy beans, rinsed and drained
1 4-ounce can chopped green chilies
1/2 cup water
1 1/2 teaspoons chili powder
1 teaspoon ground cumin
1 tablespoon sugar
1 tablespoon extra virgin olive oil
1/4 cup fat-free or light sour cream
1/4 cup chopped cilantro leaves

1 In a 3-quart saucepan, combine tomatoes, broth, beans, green chilies, water, chili powder, cumin, and sugar. Bring to boil over high heat, then reduce heat, cover tightly, and simmer 20 minutes.

2 Remove from heat, stir in oil, cover, and let stand 5 minutes to allow flavors to blend. Top each serving with 1 tablespoon sour cream and 1 tablespoon cilantro.

Try it with

1 corn tortilla topped
   with 1/4 cup shredded
   cheese, melted
3/4 cup pineapple chunks
   or 2 pineapple slices

Total meal:
  4 carb exchanges

Exchanges

2 Starch
1 Vegetable
1/2 Fat

Calories....................214
  Calories from Fat......37
Total Fat........................4 g
  Saturated Fat..............0 g
Cholesterol...................1 mg
Sodium......................954 mg
Carbohydrate.............35 g
  Dietary Fiber...............8 g
  Sugars ....12 g
Protein...........................9 g

Serving size:
   1/4 recipe

Skillet Ham with Mild Curried Apples

2 medium red apples, preferably Gala, cored and
   cut into 1/2-inch cubes
1/4 cup chopped dried apricots
   2 tablespoons dark brown sugar, packed
   2 tablespoons water
1/2 teaspoon curry powder
1/4 teaspoon vanilla
1 1/2 teaspoons reduced-fat margarine
   8 ounces extra lean ham slices

1 In a small saucepan, combine apples, apricots, brown sugar, water, and curry. Bring to a boil over medium high heat, then reduce heat, cover tightly, and simmer 5 minutes or until apples are just tender, stirring occasionally.

2 Remove from heat, stir in vanilla and reduced-fat margarine, cover tightly, and let stand 5 minutes to allow flavors to blend.

3 Place a 12-inch nonstick skillet over medium high heat until hot. Coat skillet with cooking spray, and cook ham on each side 1–2 minutes or until beginning to brown richly, working in 2 batches.

4 Serve ham slices with apple mixture alongside.

Try it with

1 cup cooked couscous
   or brown or white rice
2 tablespoons finely
   chopped red or green
   bell pepper
3/4 cup steamed broccoli
   florets
1 teaspoon reduced-fat
   margarine

Total meal:
   4 carb exchanges

Exchanges

2 Very Lean Meat
1 1/2 Fruit
1/2 Fat

Calories 173
   Calories from Fat 37
Total Fat .... 4 g
   Saturated Fat .... 1 g
Cholesterol .... 32 mg
Sodium .... 765 mg
Carbohydrate .... 20 g
   Dietary Fiber .... 2 g
   Sugars .... 17 g
Protein .... 15 g

Jerked Pork with Nectarine–Dried Cherry Salsa

Serves: 4

Serving size:
 1/4 recipe

1 pound pork tenderloin

1 tablespoon jerk seasoning

2 medium nectarines, finely chopped

1/2 cup dried cherries or cranberries

2 teaspoons orange zest

1/4 cup orange juice

1 teaspoon grated gingerroot

1 jalapeño pepper, seeded and finely chopped, or 1/4 teaspoon dried red pepper flakes

1 Preheat oven to 425°F.

2 Place pork on a nonstick baking sheet. Sprinkle evenly with jerk seasoning. Bake 22–24 minutes or until lightly pink in center.

3 Meanwhile, in a medium mixing bowl, combine remaining ingredients.

4 Place pork on cutting board and let stand 5 minutes before thinly slicing. Serve with salsa.

Try it with

2/3 cup cooked brown or white rice

2 tablespoons green onion

1/2 cup steamed snow or sugar snap peas

1 teaspoon light soy sauce

Total meal:
 4 carb exchanges

Exchanges

3 Lean Meat

1 1/2 Fruit

Calories 241

 Calories from Fat 40

Total Fat .... 4 g

 Saturated Fat .... 1 g

Cholesterol .... 65 mg

Sodium .... 262 mg

Carbohydrate .... 26 g

 Dietary Fiber .... 2 g

 Sugars .... 19 g

Protein .... 25 g

Cumin Pork and Sweet Potatoes with Spiced Butter

1 pound sweet potatoes, peeled and cut into
   1/2-inch cubes
2 tablespoons reduced-fat margarine
3 tablespoons dark brown sugar, packed
1/2 teaspoon grated orange rind
1/4 teaspoon vanilla, butter, and nut flavoring or
   1/2 teaspoon vanilla
1/8 teaspoon ground nutmeg
1/2 teaspoon ground cumin
1/4 teaspoon salt
1/4 teaspoon black pepper
   Paprika to taste
4 4-ounce boneless pork cutlets, fat trimmed

1 Place a collapsible steamer basket in a 3-quart saucepan. Add 2 cups water, arrange potatoes in basket, and bring to a boil over high heat. Cover tightly and steam 10–12 minutes or until potatoes are just tender.

2 Meanwhile, in a small bowl, combine reduced-fat margarine, brown sugar, orange rind, vanilla, and nutmeg and set aside.

3 Sprinkle cumin, salt, pepper, and paprika evenly over one side of each pork cutlet. Place a 12-inch nonstick skillet over medium heat until hot. Coat skillet with cooking spray, add pork (seasoned side down), and cook 5 minutes. Turn and cook 4 more minutes or until pork is no longer pink in center.

4 When potatoes are cooked, remove from steamer basket and discard water. Add potatoes back to pot, add margarine mixture, and mix gently with a rubber spatula to coat while still keeping potatoes in cubes.

Try it with

1 1-ounce low-fat corn muffin
1/2 cup shredded purple cabbage
1 tablespoon reduced-fat salad dressing
1 cup cooked yellow squash

Total meal:
   4 carb exchanges

Exchanges

2 Starch
3 Lean Meat

Calories	293
Calories from Fat	63
Total Fat	7 g
Saturated Fat	2 g
Cholesterol	65 mg
Sodium	243 mg
Carbohydrate	32 g
Dietary Fiber	3 g
Sugars	20 g
Protein	25 g

Shrimp with Chipotle Cocktail Sauce

Serves: 4

Serving size:
 1/4 recipe

1 pound raw unpeeled medium shrimp
1 teaspoon Creole seasoning
1/3 cup ketchup
1 tablespoon bottled prepared horseradish
1 tablespoon lemon juice
1 chipotle chile pepper in adobo sauce, chopped and mashed with a fork
1 medium lemon, quartered

1 Peel shrimp. Place a 12-inch nonstick skillet over medium heat until hot. Coat skillet with cooking spray, add shrimp and Creole seasoning, and cook 4 minutes or until opaque in center.

2 Remove from heat, drain, and cool completely. To cool quickly, place shrimp on a baking sheet in a single layer and let stand 5–10 minutes.

3 Meanwhile, in a small mixing bowl, combine remaining ingredients.

4 To serve, place equal amount of shrimp on 4 dinner plates. Serve with 2 tablespoons ketchup mixture and lemon wedges.

Try it with

1 large ear of corn
1 1/2 teaspoons reduced-fat margarine
1 cup shredded cabbage
2 tablespoons light mayonnaise
8 salt-free saltine-style crackers

Total meal:
 4 carb exchanges

Exchanges

2 Very Lean Meat
1/2 Carbohydrate

Calories 102
 Calories from Fat 9
Total Fat .... 1 g
 Saturated Fat .... 0 g
Cholesterol .... 145 mg
Sodium .... 1032 mg
Carbohydrate .... 7 g
 Dietary Fiber .... 0 g
 Sugars .... 3 g
Protein .... 16 g

Fresh Ginger-Barbecued Drumsticks

Try it with

6 ounces baked potato
1 tablespoon reduced-
  fat margarine
1/2 cup steamed broccoli
  florets seasoned with
  butter spray and fresh
  lemon
1/3 cup blanched carrots,
  chilled
1 tablespoon reduced-
  fat salad dressing

Total meal:
  4 carb exchanges

3 tablespoons dark brown sugar, packed
1/4 cup ketchup
  1 tablespoon Worcestershire sauce
  1 tablespoon light soy sauce
  1 tablespoon cider vinegar
  1 teaspoon grated gingerroot
1/4 teaspoon dried red pepper flakes, optional
  8 chicken drumsticks, skinned, rinsed, and
    patted dry

1 Preheat broiler.

2 In a small mixing bowl, combine all ingredients except drumsticks and mix well. Reserve 1/4 cup sauce in a separate dish.

3 Coat a broiler rack and pan with cooking spray and add chicken. Broil 12–15 minutes or until no longer pink in center, turning and basting occasionally with sauce.

4 Remove from broiler and spoon reserved 1/4 cup sauce evenly over all.

Exchanges
2 Lean Meat
1 Carbohydrate

Calories 211
  Calories from Fat 46
Total Fat .... 5 g
  Saturated Fat .... 1 g
Cholesterol .... 78 mg
Sodium .... 454 mg
Carbohydrate .... 15 g
  Dietary Fiber .... 0 g
  Sugars .... 13 g
Protein .... 25 g

Creamy Baked Chicken with Crunchy Corn Bread Topping

Serves: 4

Serving size:
  1 cup

4 4-ounce boneless skinless chicken breasts, rinsed
  and patted dry
1/2 cup finely chopped green onion
  1 4-ounce container diced pimiento
  1 10 3/4-ounce can 98% fat-free cream of
  chicken soup
1/4 cup light sour cream
  1 cup frozen green peas, thawed
  2 ounces corn bread stuffing (1 cup)

1 Preheat oven to 400°F.

2 Coat a 9-inch glass pie pan with cooking spray
  and arrange chicken in bottom of pan. Top with
green onion and pimiento.

3 Combine soup and sour cream in a small bowl
  and spoon evenly over chicken. Arrange peas
around outer edges of pan and sprinkle stuffing
evenly over all.

4 Bake uncovered 30 minutes or until chicken is
  no longer pink in center.

Try it with

1/2 cup steamed cubed
  sweet potatoes
  1 teaspoon reduced-fat
  margarine
3/4 cup steamed green
  beans seasoned with
  butter spray
3/4 cup pineapple chunks
  or 2 pineapple slices

Total meal:
  4 carb exchanges

Exchanges
2 Starch
4 Very Lean Meat

Calories 290
  Calories from Fat 46
Total Fat .... 5 g
  Saturated Fat .... 2 g
Cholesterol .... 75 mg
Sodium .... 583 mg
Carbohydrate .... 27 g
  Dietary Fiber .... 4 g
  Sugars .... 5 g
Protein .... 32 g

Serves: 4

Serving size:
1 1/4 cups

Rustic Cajun Chicken and Sausage Rice

6 ounces 50% less fat pork sausage
16 ounces frozen mixed pepper stir-fry, thawed
1/2 cup chopped onion
3/4 cup sliced celery
1/2 teaspoon dried thyme leaves
1 cup water
2 bay leaves
1/2 cup uncooked white rice
1/2 teaspoon paprika
8 ounces boneless skinless chicken breast meat, cut into bite-sized pieces
Hot pepper sauce to taste

■
Try it with

1 cooked artichoke
  seasoned with fresh
  lemon and butter spray
1 medium tomato, sliced
1 ounce French bread
1 teaspoon reduced-fat
  margarine

Total meal:
  4 carb exchanges

1 Place a 12-inch nonstick skillet over medium high heat until hot. Add sausage and cook until no longer pink, breaking up larger pieces while stirring. Remove from skillet and set aside.

2 Add pepper stir-fry, onion, celery, and thyme to pan residue and cook 3–4 minutes, stirring frequently. Increase heat to high, add water and bay leaves, and bring to a boil. Add rice and paprika and return to a boil. Reduce heat, cover tightly, and simmer 15 minutes.

3 Add chicken and cook 5 more minutes or until chicken is no longer pink in center. Remove skillet from heat and stir in sausage and hot pepper sauce. Cover and let stand 5 minutes to absorb flavors.

Exchanges

1 1/2 Starch
2 Lean Meat
1 Vegetable
1/2 Fat

Calories 284
  Calories from Fat 90
Total Fat .... 10 g
  Saturated Fat .... 3 g
Cholesterol .... 61 mg
Sodium .... 327 mg
Carbohydrate .... 27 g
  Dietary Fiber .... 2 g
  Sugars .... 4 g
Protein .... 23 g

Seared Sirloin Steaks with Sour Cream Potatoes

Serves: 4

Serving size:
  1/4 recipe

1 pound boneless sirloin steak, about 1 inch thick
2 garlic cloves, halved
1 pound red potatoes, sliced
2 medium yellow onions, chopped
1/2 cup light sour cream
  2 tablespoons grated Parmesan cheese
  2 tablespoons fat-free milk
3/4 teaspoon salt, divided
1/4 cup chopped parsley
  Black pepper to taste

1 Cut steak in four even pieces. Rub both sides of each steak with garlic halves, then discard garlic and set steaks aside.

2 Place a collapsible steamer basket in a 3-quart saucepan. Add 2 cups water, arrange potatoes and onion in basket, and bring to a boil over high heat. Cover tightly and steam 6–8 minutes or until potatoes are just tender.

3 Meanwhile, in a small bowl, combine sour cream, Parmesan cheese, milk, and 1/2 teaspoon salt and set aside.

4 Place potatoes in a shallow pasta bowl or serving platter and spoon sour cream mixture evenly over potatoes. Sprinkle with parsley and black pepper. Cover with a sheet of foil to keep warm.

5 Place a 12-inch nonstick skillet over high heat until hot. Coat skillet with cooking spray, add steaks, and cook 3 minutes. Turn steaks and cook 3 minutes. Reduce heat to medium, turn steaks again, and cook 2–6 minutes longer or until steak is done to your liking. Sprinkle steaks with remaining 1/4 teaspoon salt and pepper.

Try it with

1 cup cooked carrots seasoned with butter spray
1/2 cup diced cucumber
1/2 cup diced tomato
1/4 cup diced green bell pepper
  2 tablespoons reduced-fat salad dressing

Total meal:
  4 carb exchanges

Exchanges

1 1/2 Starch
3 Lean Meat
1 Vegetable

Calories 309
  Calories from Fat 79
Total Fat .... 9 g
  Saturated Fat .... 4 g
Cholesterol .... 78 mg
Sodium .... 581 mg
Carbohydrate .... 29 g
  Dietary Fiber .... 3 g
  Sugars .... 7 g
Protein .... 29 g

Serves: 4

Serving size:
1 burger

![gray square icon]
Try it with

1/2 cup baked beans
1 cup shredded cabbage
2 tablespoons reduced-
   fat salad dressing

Total meal:
   4 carb exchanges

Exchanges

2 Starch
3 Lean Meat

Calories....................331
   Calories from Fat......91
Total Fat.......................10 g
   Saturated Fat...............4 g
Cholesterol.................79 mg
Sodium.......................665 mg
Carbohydrate.............27 g
   Dietary Fiber................2 g
   Sugars.........................7 g
Protein.........................30 g

Hometown Cheeseburgers

1 pound 96% extra-lean ground beef
3 tablespoons steak sauce
2 tablespoons finely chopped yellow onion
1/2 teaspoon minced bottled garlic, or 2 garlic cloves,
   minced
2 tablespoons chopped parsley leaves
2 slices reduced-fat American cheese, cut in half
   diagonally
4 small hamburger buns, toasted
4 lettuce leaves
1 small tomato, cut in 4 slices

1 In a medium mixing bowl, combine ground beef, steak sauce, onion, garlic, and parsley. Blend well and form into 4 even patties.

2 Place a 12-inch nonstick skillet over medium heat until hot. Coat skillet with cooking spray, add beef patties, and cook 4 minutes. Turn patties and cook 3 minutes or until burgers are done to your liking.

3 Remove from heat, top beef patties with cheese slices, cover tightly, and let stand 1 minute to allow cheese to melt.

4 Serve on toasted buns with lettuce and tomato slices.

BREAKFASTS

5

Carb Exchanges

Hot and Steaming
Sweet Plum Oatmeal

Try it with

2 Canadian bacon slices,
   heated
1 cup fat-free milk

Total meal:
   5 carb exchanges

4	cups water
2	cups quick-cooking oats
20	orange essence dried plums, chopped
2	tablespoons reduced-fat margarine
1 1/2	teaspoons ground cinnamon
2	tablespoons dark brown sugar, packed
1	teaspoon vanilla or 1/2 teaspoon vanilla, butter, and nut flavoring
1/8	teaspoon salt

1 In a medium saucepan, bring water to boil over high heat and stir in oats and plums. Reduce heat and simmer 1 minute, stirring frequently.

2 Remove from heat, stir in remaining ingredients, cover tightly, and let stand 5 minutes to absorb flavors and thicken slightly.

Exchanges

2 Starch
2 Fruit
1 Fat

Calories 316
   Calories from Fat 50
Total Fat ....6 g
   Saturated Fat ....1 g
Cholesterol ....0 mg
Sodium ....123 mg
Carbohydrate.............60 g
   Dietary Fiber................8 g
   Sugars ....20 g
Protein...........................8 g

Apple Pumpkin Coffee Cake

Serves: 12

Serving size:
 1 piece

1 18-ounce box spice or carrot cake mix
5 large egg whites or 3/4 cup egg substitute
1 cup water
1 cup canned solid pumpkin
2 ounces pecan chips
8 ounces Gala apples, peeled and very thinly sliced
1 cup apple juice
2 teaspoons cornstarch

1 Preheat oven to 350°F. Coat a springform or bundt pan with cooking spray.

2 In a medium mixing bowl, combine cake mix, egg whites, water, and pumpkin. Using an electric mixer on low speed, beat until moistened, about 30 seconds. Scrape sides and beat on medium speed 2 minutes or until smooth.

3 Sprinkle bottom of pan with pecans and lay out apple slices accordion fashion. Carefully pour batter over apples and bake 1 hour or until a wooden toothpick comes out clean.

4 Meanwhile, in a small saucepan, combine apple juice and cornstarch and stir until completely dissolved. Bring to a boil and cook 1 minute or until thickened. Remove from heat and cool completely.

5 When cake is done, remove from oven and cool 5 minutes on a wire rack. Inverting onto a serving platter, remove sides and bottom of springform pan, and pour apple glaze over all.

Try it with

2 ounces extra-lean ham
 slices, heated
1 cup fat-free milk
1 small banana

Total meal:
 5 carb exchanges

Exchanges

1/2 Fat
3 Carbohydrate

Calories	240
Calories from Fat	60
Total Fat	7 g
Saturated Fat	1 g
Cholesterol	0 mg
Sodium	295 mg
Carbohydrate	43 g
Dietary Fiber	2 g
Sugars	26 g
Protein	3 g

Serves: 4

Serving size:
  1 cup

Tropical Fruits with Fresh Ginger

1 medium ripe mango, peeled, seed removed, and cut in cubes
2 cups fresh pineapple chunks
1 small banana, cut in 1/4-inch slices
1/3 cup orange juice
2 teaspoons grated gingerroot or to taste

Place all ingredients in a medium bowl and mix gently, yet thoroughly.

Try it with

2 ounces bagel (1/2 large), toasted
1 ounce reduced-fat cream cheese
2 slices Canadian bacon, heated
3/4 cup fat-free milk

Total meal:
  5 carb exchanges

Exchanges

2 Fruit

Calories	125
Calories from Fat	6
Total Fat	1 g
Saturated Fat	0 g
Cholesterol	0 mg
Sodium	3 mg
Carbohydrate	32 g
Dietary Fiber	3 g
Sugars	26 g
Protein	1 g

Breakfast Blast in a Glass

Serves: 4

Serving size:
  1 cup

1 small banana, sliced
2 cups low-fat vanilla yogurt
2 cups frozen unsweetened peaches, slightly thawed

Place ingredients in a blender and blend until smooth.

Try it with

1 veggie breakfast patty
2 slices raisin bread toast
2 teaspoons reduced-fat
  margarine

Total meal:
  5 carb exchanges

Exchanges
2 Fruit
1/2 Fat
1 Carbohydrate

Calories 220
  Calories from Fat 20
Total Fat ....2 g
  Saturated Fat ....1 g
Cholesterol ....7 mg
Sodium ....84 mg
Carbohydrate ....47 g
  Dietary Fiber ....3 g
  Sugars ....38 g
Protein ....7 g

Start-the-Day Berry Parfait

1 1/2 cups fresh or frozen unsweetened blueberries
   1/4 cup raspberry 100% fruit spread
   1/4 teaspoon ground cinnamon
2 1/2 cups sliced fresh strawberries
   2 teaspoons grated orange rind
   1 teaspoon grated gingerroot
   2 cups low-fat vanilla yogurt
   1 cup low-fat granola

Try it with

2 slices cooked bacon
2 ounces bagel (1/2 large), toasted
1 teaspoon reduced-fat margarine

Total meal:
   5 carb exchanges

1 If using frozen blueberries, place in a colander and run under cold water 10–15 seconds to thaw quickly, but still keep firm. Drain on paper towels and set aside.

2 Place fruit spread in a small microwave-safe bowl and microwave on HIGH setting 5–10 seconds or until fruit spread has liquefied slightly.

3 In a medium bowl, combine cinnamon, strawberries, blueberries, grated orange rind, gingerroot, and fruit spread.

4 Spoon 1/4 cup yogurt in the bottom of 4 clear glasses, wine goblets, or dessert bowls. Top with 1/2 cup fruit mixture, then 2 tablespoons granola. Repeat all layers once.

Exchanges

1 Starch
2 Fruit
1/2 Fat
1 Carbohydrate

Calories.....................295
   Calories from Fat.....31
Total Fat.........................3 g
   Saturated Fat...............1 g
Cholesterol...................7 mg
Sodium......................148 mg
Carbohydrate.............62 g
   Dietary Fiber................5 g
   Sugars........................41 g
Protein............................8 g

Sausage and Potato Skillet Toss

Serves: 4

Serving size:
  1 1/4 cups

1/2 of a 20-ounce package refrigerated
     diced potatoes with onion
   2 teaspoons extra virgin olive oil
     Paprika to taste
   6 ounces 50% less fat breakfast pork sausage
   1 cup sliced mushrooms
   1 medium green bell pepper, chopped
   1 medium yellow onion, chopped
1/4 cup chopped parsley leaves
1/2 teaspoon salt

1 Preheat oven to 475°F.

2 Coat a nonstick baking sheet with cooking
  spray, add potatoes, drizzle oil over them, and
shake pan gently to coat.

3 Sprinkle even layer of potatoes with paprika and
  bake 5 minutes. Stir and bake 5 more minutes
or until potatoes are golden.

4 Meanwhile, place a 12-inch nonstick skillet
  over medium high heat until hot. Cook sausage
5–6 minutes or until thoroughly brown, stirring to
break up large pieces. Set sausage aside on separate
plate lined with paper towels.

5 Add mushrooms, bell pepper, and onion to pan
  residue and cook 5 minutes or until onion is
translucent, stirring frequently. Add sausage,
potatoes, parsley, and salt and stir.

Try it with

1 whole English muffin,
  halved and toasted
2 teaspoons reduced-fat
  margarine
1 cup orange juice

Total meal:
  5 carb exchanges

Exchanges

1 Starch
1 Medium-Fat Meat
1 Vegetable
1 Fat

Calories 219
  Calories from Fat 102
Total Fat .... 11 g
  Saturated Fat .... 3 g
Cholesterol .... 29 mg
Sodium .... 698 mg
Carbohydrate .... 22 g
  Dietary Fiber .... 3 g
  Sugars .... 3 g
Protein .... 11 g

Weekend Morning Bacon-Potato Casserole

1 20-ounce package refrigerated Southwest-style hash browns
1 cup shredded reduced-fat sharp cheddar cheese, divided
1/2 medium green bell pepper, finely chopped
1/2 cup finely chopped green onion
1 cup egg substitute
1/4 cup fat-free milk
4 reduced-sodium bacon slices

1 Preheat oven to 350°F. Coat an ovenproof casserole dish or a 9-inch deep-dish glass pie pan with cooking spray.

2 Place potatoes on dish bottom and top with 1/2 cup cheese, bell pepper, and onion. Pour egg substitute and milk evenly over all. Cover tightly and bake 45 minutes.

3 Meanwhile, place layers of paper towels on a microwave-safe plate, arrange bacon slices on top in a single layer, and cover with a paper towel. Microwave on HIGH setting 3–4 minutes or until crisp. Cool slightly, crumble into small pieces, and set aside.

4 After casserole has baked 45 minutes, top with remaining cheese and bacon and bake 5 minutes longer or until knife inserted comes out clean. Let stand 10 minutes for easier slicing and to allow flavors to blend.

Try it with

1 3/4 cups strawberries
1 slice whole wheat toast
1 tablespoon 100% fruit spread
1 cup fat-free milk

Total meal:
  5 carb exchanges

Exchanges

2 Starch
2 Lean Meat
1/2 Fat

Calories	283
Calories from Fat	82
Total Fat	9 g
Saturated Fat	5 g
Cholesterol	25 mg
Sodium	769 mg
Carbohydrate	29 g
Dietary Fiber	4 g
Sugars	4 g
Protein	20 g

LUNCHES

5
Carb Exchanges

Skillet Ranch Soup

1 1/2 cups chopped yellow onion
  2 medium green bell peppers, chopped
  1 15-ounce can navy beans, rinsed and drained
  1 14-ounce can low-fat reduced-sodium
    chicken broth
1/2 cup water
1/2 of a .4-ounce packet dry ranch-style salad
    dressing mix
  1 tablespoon extra virgin olive oil
  2 teaspoons ground cumin
  1 medium lime, cut in 4 wedges
1/4 cup finely chopped tomatoes
1/4 cup fat-free sour cream

Try it with

  1 6-inch corn tortilla
    topped with 1/4 cup
    shredded cheese,
    melted
1 1/4 cups strawberries
  2/3 cup fat-free
    artificially
    sweetened fruit-
    flavored yogurt

Total meal:
  5 carb exchanges

1 Place a 12-inch nonstick skillet over medium high heat until hot. Coat skillet with cooking spray, add onion, and cook 4 minutes or until onion is translucent, stirring occasionally.

2 Add bell pepper, beans, broth, water, and salad dressing mix. Increase heat to high and bring to a boil. Reduce heat, cover tightly, and simmer 15 minutes. Remove from heat and stir in oil and cumin.

3 Spoon into 4 individual soup bowls. Squeeze lime juice over soup, sprinkle each serving with 1 tablespoon tomatoes, and top with 1 tablespoon sour cream.

Exchanges

1 1/2 Starch
2 Vegetable
1 Fat

Calories 210
  Calories from Fat 39

Total Fat .... 4 g
  Saturated Fat .... 0 g
Cholesterol .... 1 mg
Sodium .... 702 mg
Carbohydrate .... 35 g
  Dietary Fiber .... 7 g
  Sugars .... 9 g
Protein .... 10 g

Ham and Swiss Scallion Quesadillas

Serves: 4

Serving size:
  2 quesadilla wedges

4 ounces Swiss cheese, torn in small pieces
4 10-inch flour tortillas
4 ounces extra-lean ham, thinly sliced and chopped
1/2 medium red bell pepper, finely chopped
1/2 cup finely chopped green onion

1 Preheat oven to warm. Place 1/4 of the cheese on 1/2 of each tortilla.

2 Top each cheese portion with 1 1/2 ounces ham, 2 tablespoons bell pepper, and 2 tablespoons onion. Fold over tortillas and press down gently to make them adhere.

3 Place a 12-inch nonstick skillet over medium heat until hot. Coat both sides of two tortillas with cooking spray and place in skillet. Cook 2 minutes, turn, and cook 1–2 minutes longer or until cheese has melted and tortillas are golden.

4 Remove from heat and place in oven to keep warm. Repeat with remaining two tortillas. Using a serrated knife, cut tortillas in half, beginning on the folded side for easier cutting.

Try it with

1 cup spinach leaves
1/2 cup chopped tomatoes
2 tablespoons reduced-fat salad dressing
1/2 large ear of corn
3/4 cup diced cantaloupe

Total meal:
  5 carb exchanges

Exchanges
3 Starch
2 Medium-Fat Meat

Calories 391
  Calories from Fat....130
Total Fat .... 14 g
  Saturated Fat .... 7 g
Cholesterol .... 42 mg
Sodium .... 786 mg
Carbohydrate .... 43 g
  Dietary Fiber................ 3 g
  Sugars.......................... 3 g
Protein .... 22 g

Serves: 4

Serving size:
   1 1/2 cups

Retro Macaroni Salad with Ham

6 ounces uncooked dry elbow macaroni
4 ounces extra lean ham, chopped
1 cup finely chopped green bell pepper
3/4 cup thinly sliced celery
1/4 cup finely chopped red or yellow onion
3 tablespoons sweet pickle relish
1/3 cup light mayonnaise

1 Cook macaroni according to directions on package, omitting any salt or fats.

2 Meanwhile, in a medium mixing bowl, combine remaining ingredients. Mix well and set aside.

3 Drain cooked macaroni in colander and run under cold water until completely cooled. Shake off excess liquid.

4 Add macaroni to ham mixture and mix gently, yet thoroughly.

Try it with

1 small apple
1 granola bar

Total meal:
   5 carb exchanges

Exchanges

2 1/2 Starch
1 Lean Meat
1 Fat

Calories 301
   Calories from Fat 82
Total Fat .... 9 g
   Saturated Fat .... 2 g
Cholesterol .... 23 mg
Sodium .... 652 mg
Carbohydrate .... 41 g
   Dietary Fiber .... 2 g
   Sugars .... 7 g
Protein .... 13 g

Tuscan Orzo and White Bean Salad

Serves: 4

Serving size:
1 cup

6 ounces uncooked dry orzo pasta
12 kalamata olives, pitted and coarsely chopped
3 tablespoons capers, drained
2 tablespoons finely chopped parsley
2 tablespoons cider vinegar
2 tablespoons extra virgin olive oil
1 tablespoon dried basil leaves
1 garlic clove, minced
1 15.5-ounce can navy beans
4 romaine lettuce leaves

1 Cook pasta according to directions on package, omitting any salt or fats.

2 Meanwhile, in a medium mixing bowl, combine olives, capers, parsley, vinegar, oil, basil, and garlic.

3 Place beans in a colander and drain cooked pasta and water over beans. Run pasta mixture under cool water until completely cooled.

4 Shake off excess liquid and add pasta and beans to olive mixture. Mix gently, yet thoroughly.

5 Place a lettuce leaf on each plate and top each with 1 cup pasta mixture.

Try it with

3 tomato slices
17 seedless grapes

Total meal:
5 carb exchanges

Exchanges
3 1/2 Starch
1 1/2 Fat

Calories 342
   Calories from Fat 81
Total Fat .... 9 g
   Saturated Fat .... 1 g
Cholesterol .... 0 mg
Sodium .... 438 mg
Carbohydrate .... 53 g
   Dietary Fiber .... 7 g
   Sugars .... 4 g
Protein .... 12 g

Black Bean, Mozzarella, and Yellow Rice Salad

Serves: 4

Serving size:
1 1/2 cups

1 boil-in-bag rice packet or 2 cups cooked rice
1/2 teaspoon turmeric, optional
1 15.5-ounce can black beans, rinsed and drained
1 poblano chili pepper, finely chopped
1 1/2 cups sweet grape cherry tomatoes, quartered
4 ounces part-skim mozzarella cheese, cut in
   1/4-inch cubes
1/4 cup chopped cilantro leaves
1/4 cup lime juice
3/4 teaspoon salt
1/4 teaspoon dried red pepper flakes
1 tablespoon extra virgin olive oil

Try it with

1 cup shredded cabbage
2 tablespoons reduced-fat
   salad dressing
1 medium orange

Total meal:
   5 carb exchanges

1 Cook rice according to directions on package, omitting any salt or fats, but adding turmeric to the water.

2 Meanwhile, in a large mixing bowl, combine remaining ingredients except oil.

3 To cool rice quickly, place rice on a baking sheet in a thin layer and let stand 5 minutes. Add rice to bean mixture and mix gently. Add oil and mix gently again.

Exchanges
2 1/2 Starch
1 Medium-Fat Meat
1 Vegetable
1/2 Fat

Calories 323
   Calories from Fat 78
Total Fat ....9 g
   Saturated Fat ....4 g
Cholesterol ....16 mg
Sodium ....672 mg
Carbohydrate ....46 g
   Dietary Fiber ....8 g
   Sugars ....5 g
Protein ....16 g

Veggie Sloppy Joes

Serves: 8

Serving size:
   1 sandwich

1 pound 96% extra-lean ground beef
1 14.5-ounce can diced tomatoes with peppers and onion, drained
1 cup frozen mixed vegetables, thawed
1/2 medium green bell pepper, chopped
3 tablespoons ketchup
1 teaspoon ground cumin
8 small hamburger buns, toasted

1 Place a 12-inch nonstick skillet over medium high heat until hot. Cook beef 3–4 minutes or until no longer pink in center, stirring constantly.

2 Add tomatoes, mixed vegetables, and bell pepper. Stir occasionally until mixture begins to simmer, then reduce heat, cover tightly, and simmer 15 minutes or until vegetables are tender.

3 Remove from heat, stir in ketchup and cumin, cover, and let stand 5 minutes to thicken slightly and allow flavors to blend. Serve on buns. This dish freezes well: freeze 1/2 cup individual servings in small plastic bags.

Try it with

15 fat-free potato chips
2/3 cup fat-free artificially sweetened fruit-flavored yogurt
1 1/4 cups watermelon cubes

Total meal:
   5 carb exchanges

Exchanges

2 Starch
1 Lean Meat
1 Vegetable

Calories......................231
   Calories from Fat......37
Total Fat........................4 g
   Saturated Fat..............1 g
Cholesterol.................32 mg
Sodium......................537 mg
Carbohydrate............30 g
   Dietary Fiber................3 g
   Sugars.........................8 g
Protein........................18 g

Serves: 6

Serving size:
  2 cups

Great Big Salad

Try it with

1 cup 98% fat-free
  cream of chicken
  soup (made with
  fat-free milk)
1 medium peach
1/12 angel food cake

Total meal:
  5 carb exchanges

Exchanges

1/2 Starch
2 Lean Meat
1 Vegetable

Calories 193
  Calories from Fat 72
Total Fat .... 8 g
  Saturated Fat .... 4 g
Cholesterol .... 51 mg
Sodium .... 513 mg
Carbohydrate .... 11 g
  Dietary Fiber .... 1 g
  Sugars .... 4 g
Protein .... 18 g

    2 ounces French bread, cut in 1/2-inch cubes
1/2 cup fat-free Italian salad dressing
    1 tablespoon Dijon mustard
1 1/2 tablespoons dried basil leaves
    1 10-ounce bag chopped romaine lettuce
    1 medium red bell pepper, thinly sliced
1/2 cup thinly sliced red onion
    9 ounces frozen cooked diced chicken, thawed
    4 ounces feta cheese seasoned with basil and
        sun-dried tomatoes, crumbled

1 Preheat oven to 350°F.

2 Place bread cubes on baking sheet and bake
12 minutes or until golden. Remove from heat
and let cool completely.

3 Meanwhile, in a small bowl, whisk together
dressing, mustard, and basil and set aside.

4 In a large salad bowl, combine romaine, bell
pepper, onion, and chicken. Add dressing and
toss gently, yet thoroughly, to coat. Add croutons,
toss, and top with feta.

DINNERS

5
Carb Exchanges

Vegetable Pilaf with Toasted Nuts

1 cup water
1/2 cup brown rice
  3 ounces slivered (not sliced) almonds or peanuts
  2 medium carrots, peeled and cut into 1/4-inch cubes
  2 medium yellow onions, chopped
  1 medium red bell pepper, chopped
1/4 cup water
1/3 cup raisins
  1 teaspoon ground cinnamon
1/2 teaspoon ground cumin
3/4 teaspoon salt

1 In a small saucepan, bring water to a boil. Add rice, reduce heat, cover tightly, and simmer 25–30 minutes or until rice is done.

2 Meanwhile, place a 12-inch nonstick skillet over medium high heat until hot. Add nuts and cook 3 minutes or until beginning to brown, stirring frequently. Remove from heat and set aside on a separate plate.

3 Return skillet to medium high heat and coat skillet with cooking spray. Add carrots, onion, and bell pepper. Spray vegetables lightly with cooking spray and cook 8 minutes or until onion begins to brown, stirring frequently.

4 Remove from heat and add 1/4 cup water, raisins, cinnamon, cumin, and salt. Cover tightly to keep warm while rice is cooking. To serve, stir nuts into vegetable mixture and spoon over rice.

Italian Eggplant and Tomato Ragout

Serves: 4

Serving size:
   1 cup eggplant plus
   3/4 cup pasta

1 medium green bell pepper, chopped
1 medium yellow onion, chopped
8 ounces eggplant, diced
1 medium zucchini, thinly sliced
1 14.5-ounce can diced tomatoes with peppers
   and onion
2 teaspoons dried basil leaves
1/4 teaspoon dried red pepper flakes, optional
6 ounces uncooked dry penne pasta
1/4 cup capers, drained
1 tablespoon extra virgin olive oil
1 cup shredded part-skim mozzarella cheese

1 Place a medium saucepot over medium high heat until hot. Coat pot with cooking spray, add bell pepper and onion, and cook 4 minutes or until onion is translucent.

2 Add eggplant, zucchini, tomatoes, basil, and red pepper flakes. Bring to a boil, reduce heat, cover tightly, and simmer 30 minutes or until eggplant is very tender, stirring occasionally.

3 Meanwhile, cook pasta according to directions on package, omitting any salt or fats.

4 Remove veggie pot from heat and stir in capers and oil. Place pasta in a shallow pasta bowl, top with veggies, and sprinkle evenly with mozzarella.

Try it with

1 cooked artichoke seasoned with butter spray and fresh lemon
1 ounce crusty French bread

Total meal:
   5 carb exchanges

Exchanges

2 Starch
1 Medium-Fat Meat
3 Vegetable
1/2 Fat

Calories 340
   Calories from Fat 82
Total Fat ....9 g
   Saturated Fat ....4 g
Cholesterol ....16 mg
Sodium ....785 mg
Carbohydrate............49 g
   Dietary Fiber...............7 g
   Sugars ....13 g
Protein........................16 g

Mediterranean Vegetable Stir-Fry with Feta

Try it with

1/2 cup cooked spinach
1/2 small whole wheat roll
17 frozen seedless grapes

Total meal:
    5 carb exchanges

Exchanges

2 Starch
2 Vegetable
2 Fat

Calories 319
    Calories from Fat....100
Total Fat ....11 g
    Saturated Fat ....4 g
Cholesterol ....15 mg
Sodium ....307 mg
Carbohydrate ....44 g
    Dietary Fiber................4 g
    Sugars...........................8 g
Protein ....11 g

  6 ounces uncooked dry rotini pasta
  1 tablespoon extra virgin olive oil, divided
  1 medium yellow onion, chopped
  1 medium green bell pepper, thinly sliced
  1 medium zucchini, quartered lengthwise, then cut
      into 2-inch pieces
  1 tablespoon dried basil leaves
  1 pint cherry tomatoes, preferably sweet grape
      variety, quartered
16 pitted kalamata olives, coarsely chopped
  3 ounces feta cheese seasoned with sun-dried
      tomatoes and basil, crumbled

1 Cook pasta according to directions on package, omitting any salt or fats.

2 Meanwhile, place a medium saucepot over medium high heat until hot. Coat pot with cooking spray and add 1 teaspoon oil.

3 Add onion, bell pepper, zucchini, and basil and cook 5–7 minutes or until zucchini is tender crisp and beginning to brown on the edges, stirring frequently.

4 Remove pot from heat and stir in tomatoes, olives, and remaining oil. Cover tightly and let stand 5 minutes to allow flavors to blend.

5 Drain pasta and place in a shallow pasta bowl, top with zucchini mixture, and sprinkle evenly with feta.

Pork with Farmhouse Corn Bread Stuffing

Serves: 4

Serving size:
  1 chop plus
  1 cup stuffing

4 4-ounce pork chops, fat trimmed
  Paprika to taste
1 teaspoon dried thyme leaves, divided
1/8 teaspoon salt
1/4 teaspoon black pepper
2 cups finely chopped yellow onion
1 cup finely chopped celery
3 cups corn bread stuffing
2 cups fat-free reduced-sodium chicken broth
2 tablespoons reduced-fat margarine

1 Preheat oven to 400°F. Sprinkle one side of the pork chops with paprika, 1/4 teaspoon thyme, salt, and pepper.

2 Place a 12-inch nonstick ovenproof skillet over high heat until hot. Coat skillet with cooking spray, add pork (seasoned side down), and cook 2 minutes to brown lightly on one side. Remove pork and set aside on separate plate.

3 Reduce heat to medium high, add onion and celery, and cook 4 minutes or until onion is translucent. Remove skillet from heat and stir in stuffing, broth, margarine, and 3/4 teaspoon thyme. Stir until just blended.

4 Top with pork chops (seasoned side up), cover tightly, and bake 15 minutes or until pork is no longer pink in center. Remove from oven and let stand 5 minutes to allow flavors to blend.

Try it with

1 cup steamed asparagus spears seasoned with butter spray and fresh lemon
1 cup spinach leaves
2 tablespoons green onion
1/4 cup mandarin oranges or strawberry slices
2 tablespoons reduced-fat salad dressing
1 cup fat-free milk

Total meal:
  5 carb exchanges

Exchanges

2 1/2 Starch
2 Lean Meat
1 Vegetable
1/2 Fat

Calories 349
  Calories from Fat 85
Total Fat .... 9 g
  Saturated Fat .... 2 g
Cholesterol .... 47 mg
Sodium .... 908 mg
Carbohydrate .... 42 g
  Dietary Fiber .... 4 g
  Sugars .... 8 g
Protein .... 23 g

Serves: 4

Serving size:
  1 chop plus
  1/2 cup noodles

Pork Chops and Egg Noodles with Cupboard Gravy

6 ounces uncooked dry no-yolk egg noodles
4 5-ounce pork chops with bone in, fat trimmed
3/4 teaspoon dried thyme leaves, divided
1/4 teaspoon black pepper
    Paprika to taste
2 medium yellow onions, thinly sliced
1 12-ounce jar chicken gravy
1 1/2 teaspoons Dijon mustard

Try it with

2/3 cup cooked lima beans
1 1/2 teaspoons reduced-fat margarine
2/3 cup blanched sliced carrots
1/4 cup chopped red or green bell pepper
2 tablespoons reduced-fat salad dressing

Total meal:
  5 carb exchanges

1 Cook noodles according to directions on package, omitting any salt or fats. Meanwhile, sprinkle one side of the pork chops with 1/2 teaspoon thyme, pepper, and paprika.

2 Place a 12-inch nonstick skillet over medium high heat until hot. Coat skillet with cooking spray, add pork (seasoned side down), and cook 2 minutes to brown lightly on one side. Remove pork and set aside on separate plate.

3 Recoat skillet with cooking spray, add onion, and cook 4 minutes or until onion is richly browned, stirring frequently. Stir in gravy, mustard, and 1/4 teaspoon thyme.

4 Add pork, browned side up. Bring gravy to a boil, then reduce heat, cover tightly, and simmer 18 minutes or until pork is tender.

5 Place pork over noodles on serving platter, scrape bottom and sides of skillet with a flat spatula, and pour gravy over pork and noodles.

Exchanges

2 1/2 Starch
2 Lean Meat
1 Vegetable

Calories 356
  Calories from Fat 64
Total Fat .... 7 g
  Saturated Fat .... 2 g
Cholesterol .... 61 mg
Sodium .... 613 mg
Carbohydrate .... 40 g
  Dietary Fiber .... 4 g
  Sugars .... 6 g
Protein .... 29 g

Chicken with Tomato-Pepper Sauce

Serves: 4

Serving size:
  1/4 recipe

6 ounces uncooked dry no-yolk egg noodles
4 4-ounce boneless skinless chicken breasts,
  rinsed and patted dry
2 medium green bell peppers, thinly sliced
1 8-ounce can tomato sauce seasoned with herbs
1 tablespoon Worcestershire sauce
1 teaspoon dried oregano leaves, optional
1 1/2 tablespoons ketchup
1 tablespoon extra virgin olive oil

1 Cook noodles according to directions on package, omitting any salt or fats.

2 Meanwhile, place a 12-inch nonstick skillet over medium high heat until hot. Coat skillet with cooking spray, add chicken, and cook 1 minute. Turn and top with bell pepper, tomato sauce, Worcestershire sauce, and oregano.

3 Bring to a boil, reduce heat, cover tightly, and simmer 15 minutes or until bell pepper is tender. Remove from heat, place chicken over noodles on serving platter, and set aside.

4 Add ketchup and oil to sauce, stir, and pour over chicken and noodles.

Try it with

3/4 cup zucchini slices
    sautéed in 1/2 tea-
    spoon olive oil
  1 cup chopped romaine
    leaves
1/2 cup quartered
    artichoke hearts
1/4 cup diced tomatoes
  2 tablespoons reduced-
    fat salad dressing
  1 ounce Italian bread

Total meal:
  5 carb exchanges

Exchanges

2 Starch
3 Very Lean Meat
2 Vegetable
1 Fat

Calories 364
  Calories from Fat 62
Total Fat ....7 g
  Saturated Fat ....1 g
Cholesterol ....68 mg
Sodium ....554 mg
Carbohydrate ....40 g
  Dietary Fiber ....4 g
  Sugars ....7 g
Protein ....32 g

Weeknight Mexicali Beef and Rice

1 boil-in-bag rice packet
12 ounces extra-lean ground beef
1 14.5-ounce can no-salt-added stewed tomatoes
1/2 of a 1.25-ounce package taco seasoning mix
1 teaspoon ground cumin
1/2 cup finely chopped green onion
1/2 cup fat-free sour cream
1/2 cup shredded reduced-fat sharp cheddar cheese

1 Cook rice according to directions on package, omitting any salt or fats.

2 Meanwhile, place a 12-inch nonstick skillet over medium high heat until hot. Add beef and cook 5–6 minutes or until no longer pink, stirring occasionally.

3 Add tomatoes, taco seasoning mix, and cumin. Bring to a boil, reduce heat, cover tightly, and simmer 5 minutes.

4 Place rice on a serving platter or shallow pasta dish, top with onion, spoon beef mixture evenly over rice, and serve with sour cream and cheddar cheese.

Try it with

1/2 cup black beans
1 tablespoon cilantro leaves with lime wedges
2/3 cup cubed mango

Total meal:
   5 carb exchanges

Exchanges

2 Starch
2 Medium-Fat Meat
2 Vegetable
1 Fat

Calories 398
   Calories from Fat 147
Total Fat .... 16 g
   Saturated Fat .... 7 g
Cholesterol .... 70 mg
Sodium .... 549 mg
Carbohydrate .... 37 g
   Dietary Fiber .... 2 g
   Sugars .... 6 g
Protein .... 24 g

Tender Eye of Round Roast with Gravy

1 2-pound eye of round beef roast
1/2 teaspoon onion powder
1/2 teaspoon garlic powder
3/4 teaspoon salt, divided
1/2 teaspoon black pepper
    Paprika to taste
1 tablespoon cornstarch

1 Preheat oven to 350°F. Place beef on baking rack in pan and sprinkle with onion powder, garlic powder, 1/2 teaspoon salt, pepper, and paprika.

2 Bake 75 minutes or until the meat thermometer reads 150°F.

3 Place meat on cutting board and let stand 10 minutes before slicing. Pour any accumulated juices from the cutting board back into the baking pan.

4 Scrape bottom of pan and pour into a small saucepan. Add enough water to the drippings to measure 1 cup liquid. Stir in cornstarch and 1/4 teaspoon salt. Stir until cornstarch dissolves.

5 Place pan over high heat and bring to a boil. Cook, stirring, until gravy thickens slightly.

Serves: 8

Serving size:
  1/8 recipe

Try it with

6 ounces baked potato
2 tablespoons fat-free sour cream
1 cup steamed green beans seasoned with butter spray
1 cup mixed greens
2 tablespoons red onion
2 ounces pear slices
1/2 ounce blue cheese
2 tablespoons reduced-fat salad dressing
1 cup fat-free milk

Total meal:
  5 carb exchanges

Exchanges
3 Lean Meat

Calories 148
  Calories from Fat 40
Total Fat ....4 g
  Saturated Fat ....2 g
Cholesterol ....57 mg
Sodium ....270 mg
Carbohydrate ....1 g
  Dietary Fiber ....0 g
  Sugars ....0 g
Protein ....24 g

Penne with Chunky Tomato Sauce

  6 ounces uncooked dry penne pasta
  8 ounces 96% extra-lean ground beef
  1 cup sliced mushrooms
  1 medium green bell pepper, chopped
  1 tablespoon dried basil leaves
  2 cups bottled spaghetti sauce
  1 teaspoon sugar
 12 kalamata olives, pitted and coarsely chopped
1/4 cup chopped fresh parsley
1/2 cup shredded part-skim mozzarella cheese
  2 tablespoons grated Parmesan cheese

1 Cook pasta according to directions on package, omitting any salt or fats.

2 Meanwhile, place a 12-inch nonstick skillet over medium high heat until hot. Cook beef 5–6 minutes or until no longer pink, stirring occasionally.

3 Add mushrooms, bell pepper, and basil. Cook 5 minutes or until peppers are tender crisp, stirring frequently. Stir in spaghetti sauce and sugar, cover tightly, and simmer 10 minutes.

4 Remove from heat, stir in olives and parsley, cover, and let stand 5 minutes to allow flavors to blend.

5 Spoon sauce over pasta and sprinkle with mozzarella and Parmesan cheeses.

Fish Filets with Lemon Parsley Whip

1 pound new potatoes, quartered
4 6-ounce lean white fish filets, such as tilapia,
   snapper, or flounder, rinsed and patted dry
1/4 teaspoon black pepper
   Paprika to taste
1/4 cup reduced-fat margarine
1/2 teaspoon grated lemon rind
 2 tablespoons finely chopped parsley
1/4 teaspoon dried dill weed
1/4 teaspoon salt
 1 medium lemon

Try it with

1 cup steamed broccoli
   florets seasoned with
   butter spray
1 hard roll
1/2 cup pineapple chunks
   or 2 pineapple rings
1/2 kiwi, peeled and cut in
   wedges
1 cup fat-free milk

Total meal:
  5 carb exchanges

1 Preheat oven to 400°F.

2 Place a collapsible steamer basket in a 3-quart saucepan. Add 2 cups water, arrange potatoes in basket, and bring to a boil. Cover tightly and steam 8–10 minutes or until potatoes are just tender.

3 Meanwhile, coat a nonstick baking pan with cooking spray, arrange filets on baking pan, sprinkle evenly with black pepper and paprika, and bake 10–12 minutes or until fish is opaque in center.

4 While fish is cooking, combine margarine, lemon rind, parsley, dill weed, and salt in a small mixing bowl. Stir until well blended and set aside.

5 Using a slotted spatula, place fish on 4 dinner plates and squeeze lemon juice evenly over all. Top with parsley whip and arrange potatoes around filets.

Exchanges
1 1/2 Starch
4 Very Lean Meat
1 Fat

Calories 313
  Calories from Fat 84
Total Fat .... 9 g
  Saturated Fat .... 2 g
Cholesterol .... 114 mg
Sodium .... 274 mg
Carbohydrate .... 23 g
  Dietary Fiber .... 2 g
  Sugars .... 2 g
Protein .... 36 g

Serves: 4

Serving size:
  1 filet

Try it with

2/3 cup cooked rice
1/2 cup cooked lima
  beans
1 teaspoon reduced-
  fat margarine
3/4 cup shredded
  cabbage
1 1/2 tablespoons
  reduced-fat salad
  dressing
1 ounce low-fat corn
  muffin
1/2 cup cantaloupe cubes

Total meal:
  5 carb exchanges

Exchanges

4 Very Lean Meat
1 Vegetable
1 Fat

Calories 221
  Calories from Fat 48
Total Fat .... 5 g
  Saturated Fat .... 0 g
Cholesterol .... 61 mg
Sodium .... 570 mg
Carbohydrate .... 6 g
  Dietary Fiber .... 2 g
  Sugars .... 3 g
Protein .... 36 g

Baked Fish with Chunky Creole Vegetable Topping

1 medium celery stalk, thinly sliced
1/2 cup finely chopped onion
1/2 cup finely chopped green bell pepper
8 ounces tomato, chopped
1/2 teaspoon dried thyme leaves
4 6-ounce lean white fish filets, such as tilapia,
  snapper, or flounder, rinsed and patted dry
  Paprika to taste
2 tablespoons reduced-fat margarine
1/4 cup chopped parsley leaves
3/4 teaspoon salt
1/8–1/4 teaspoon hot pepper sauce

1 Preheat oven to 400°F.

2 Place a 12-inch nonstick skillet over medium high heat until hot. Coat skillet with cooking spray and add celery, onion, and bell pepper. Cook 4 minutes or until onion is translucent.

3 Add tomatoes and thyme, bring to a boil, reduce heat, cover tightly, and simmer 10 minutes or until celery is tender crisp.

4 Meanwhile, coat a baking sheet with cooking spray, add fish, sprinkle lightly with paprika, and bake 12 minutes or until fish is opaque in center.

5 Remove tomato mixture from heat, stir in remaining ingredients, cover, and let stand 5 minutes to absorb flavors. Spoon topping over filets.

Seared Salmon with Pineapple Salsa

1 15.25-ounce can pineapple tidbits packed in juice, drained
1/2 cup finely chopped red bell pepper
1/4 cup finely chopped red onion
1 teaspoon grated gingerroot
1/8 teaspoon dried red pepper flakes, optional
4 4-ounce salmon filets, rinsed and patted dry (about 1 inch thick)
1/4 teaspoon dried thyme leaves
1/4 teaspoon salt
1/4 teaspoon black pepper

1 Preheat broiler.

2 In a small mixing bowl, combine pineapple, bell pepper, onion, ginger, and red pepper flakes and set aside.

3 Sprinkle filets with thyme, salt, and pepper. Place filets on a broiler pan coated with cooking spray. (If you use one big 16-ounce filet, place it skin side down on the pan.)

4 Broil 10 minutes or until fish flakes. (Remove skin from large filet and discard skin.) Serve with salsa.

Serves: 4

Serving size:
  1 filet

Try it with

2/3 cup cooked rice
  2 tablespoons green onion
1/2 cup cooked pea pods
  1 teaspoon light soy sauce
1/2 cup steamed carrots
  1 teaspoon reduced-fat margarine
1/2 pear

Total meal:
  4 carb exchanges

Exchanges
3 Lean Meat
1 Fruit

Calories 242
  Calories from Fat 88
Total Fat ....10 g
  Saturated Fat ....3 g
Cholesterol ....78 mg
Sodium ....206 mg
Carbohydrate ....13 g
  Dietary Fiber ....1 g
  Sugars ....11 g
Protein ....25 g

DESSERTS

1

Carb Exchange

Peanutty Butter Chocolate Brownie

1/4 cup creamy peanut butter
  1 tablespoon water
  1 tablespoon vegetable oil
  1 large egg
  1 egg white
1/2 of an 18.25-ounce box devil's food cake mix

1 Preheat oven to 350°F.

2 In a medium mixing bowl, combine peanut butter, water, oil, egg, and egg white. Whisk until well blended. Add cake mix and stir until just blended. This mixture will be very thick.

3 Coat the bottom only of an 8 × 8-inch non-stick baking pan. Spoon batter evenly into pan.

4 Bake 15 minutes or until wooden toothpick inserted in center comes out almost clean. (The brownies will not appear to be done; they will continue cooking as they cool.)

5 Cool on wire rack and cut into 16 squares. This recipe doubles easily.

Exchanges

1/2 Fat
1 Carbohydrate

Calories 101
  Calories from Fat 37
Total Fat .... 4 g
  Saturated Fat .... 1 g
Cholesterol .... 13 mg
Sodium .... 146 mg
Carbohydrate .... 14 g
  Dietary Fiber .... 1 g
  Sugars .... 8 g
Protein .... 2 g

Apricot-Almond Meringue Cookies

Serves: 7

Serving size:
  2 cookies

  2 large egg whites
1/4 teaspoon cream of tartar
1/8 teaspoon salt
1/2 teaspoon vanilla
1/2 teaspoon grated lemon rind
1/4 cup granulated sugar
  1 ounce sliced or slivered almonds
2 1/2 tablespoons apricot 100% fruit spread

1 Preheat oven to 275°F.

2 Place egg whites in a small bowl and beat until foamy, using an electric mixer on high speed. Add cream of tartar and salt and beat until soft peaks form. Add vanilla and lemon rind. Gradually add sugar, 1 tablespoon at a time, and beat until stiff peaks form.

3 Line a baking sheet with foil. Spoon 14 uniformly-sized mounds of egg white mixture onto sheet. Bake 1 hour. Turn off oven and leave meringues in oven 2 hours longer or until very dry. (Do not open oven door!) Remove from oven and cool completely.

4 Meanwhile, place a 10-inch nonstick skillet over medium high heat until hot. Add almonds and cook 4 minutes or until golden, stirring frequently. Remove from heat and set aside.

5 To serve, stir fruit spread vigorously until it is pliable and spoon 1/2 teaspoon on top each meringue. Top with 1 teaspoon almonds each.

6 Store remaining meringues in an airtight container at room temperature up to 3 days (add fruit and almonds at time of serving.)

Exchanges
1 Carbohydrate

Calories 70
  Calories from Fat 18
Total Fat ....2 g
  Saturated Fat ....0 g
Cholesterol ....0 mg
Sodium ....61 mg
Carbohydrate ....12 g
  Dietary Fiber ....1 g
  Sugars ....10 g
Protein ....2 g

Butterscotch Chip
Spice Cookies

1 18.25-ounce box spice cake mix
2 tablespoons margarine, softened
2 tablespoons water
1 large egg
2 egg whites
1 cup quick-cooking oats
1 cup butterscotch chips

1 Preheat oven to 350°F.

2 In a large mixing bowl, combine cake mix, margarine, water, egg, and egg whites. Using an electric mixer, beat on medium speed until blended. Add oats and beat until well blended.

3 Stir in chips. Drop by rounded tablespoons 2 inches apart onto baking sheets coated with cooking spray.

4 Bake 8 minutes or until a few air bubbles begin to appear on top of the cookies. (The cookies will not appear to be done; they will continue cooking as they cool.) Carefully remove cookies with a flat spatula and cool completely on wire rack.

Exchanges
1/2 Fat
1 Carbohydrate

Calories 82
  Calories from Fat 25
Total Fat ....3 g
  Saturated Fat ....2 g
Cholesterol ....4 mg
Sodium ....82 mg
Carbohydrate ....13 g
  Dietary Fiber ....0 g
  Sugars ....8 g
Protein ....1 g

Strawberry Wine Ice

4 cups frozen unsweetened strawberries
1 12-ounce can sugar-free ginger ale
1 cup dry white wine

1 Blend all ingredients until smooth. Place in plastic container and seal tightly with a lid.

2 Place container in freezer overnight or at least 8 hours. Scrape with a fork to create a shaved ice effect before serving.

Exchanges
1 Fruit

Calories 61
  Calories from Fat 1
Total Fat ....0 g
  Saturated Fat ....0 g
Cholesterol ....0 mg
Sodium ....16 mg
Carbohydrate ....9 g
  Dietary Fiber................2 g
  Sugars..........................7 g
Protein ....0 g

DESSERTS

2

Carb Exchanges

Serves: 4

Serving size:
  1/4 recipe

Ice Cream with Berry-Berry Sauce

1/2 cup frozen unsweetened raspberries
1/2 cup frozen unsweetened blueberries
  2 tablespoons frozen white grape juice concentrate
  1 teaspoon vanilla
  1 teaspoon ground cinnamon
  2 cups reduced-fat vanilla ice cream

1 Combine all ingredients except ice cream in a medium bowl. Stir to blend well and let stand at room temperature for 30 minutes. (You may refrigerate up to 48 hours.)

2 To serve, spoon 1/2 cup ice cream into 4 glass dessert bowls or wine goblets and spoon 2 tablespoons berry mixture over each.

Exchanges
2 Carbohydrate

Calories 147
  Calories from Fat 20
Total Fat ....2 g
  Saturated Fat ....2 g
Cholesterol ....5 mg
Sodium ....53 mg
Carbohydrate ....29 g
  Dietary Fiber ....2 g
  Sugars ....26 g
Protein ....3 g

Strawberry Lemon Mousse with Crumb Topping

Serves: 4

Serving size:
  1 cup

1 .3-ounce package sugar-free lemon gelatin
3/4 cup boiling water
1/2 cup ice cubes
  2 tablespoons lemon juice
12 ounces low-fat vanilla yogurt, divided
1/2 teaspoon grated lemon rind
16 low-fat vanilla wafers, crushed in a baggie
  1 cup strawberries, quartered

1 Combine gelatin with boiling water in a medium mixing bowl and stir until gelatin is dissolved. Add ice and lemon juice and stir until ice melts.

2 Stir in 1 cup yogurt. Spoon 1/2 cup mousse into 4 glass dessert bowls or wine goblets, cover with plastic wrap, and refrigerate until firm.

3 Add lemon rind to crushed wafers, mix well, and set aside.

4 Top each serving with 2 tablespoons yogurt, 1/4 cookie mixture, and 1/4 cup strawberries.

Exchanges
1/2 Fat
2 Carbohydrate

Calories 169
  Calories from Fat 30
Total Fat .... 3 g
  Saturated Fat .... 2 g
Cholesterol .... 5 mg
Sodium .... 146 mg
Carbohydrate .... 30 g
  Dietary Fiber .... 1 g
  Sugars .... 22 g
Protein .... 6 g

Homestyle Peach Tartlets

1 refrigerated pie crust dough, at room
  temperature
8 ounces frozen unsweetened peach slices,
  thawed or any frozen berry
1/4 cup sugar
1 tablespoon cornstarch
1/4 teaspoon ground cinnamon
1/4 teaspoon vanilla, butter, and nut flavoring or
  1/2 teaspoon vanilla
1 1/2 cups reduced-fat artificially sweetened ice cream

1 Preheat oven to 450°F.

2 Unfold pie dough on a work surface or cutting
  board. Using a 3-inch biscuit cutter, cut dough
into 10 circles. Roll out remaining dough pieces
and cut into 2 additional circles.

3 Prick circles with a fork in several areas, about
  5 times per circle. Place each circle in a muffin
tin and bake 7 minutes or until lightly golden.
Carefully remove tartlets from tin and cool on a
wire rack.

4 Meanwhile, in a 12-inch nonstick skillet, combine peaches, sugar, cornstarch, and cinnamon.
Bring to a boil over high heat and boil 45–60 seconds or until thickened slightly, stirring frequently,
scraping bottom and sides of skillet.

5 Remove skillet from heat and stir in vanilla
  flavoring.

6 To serve, spoon equal amounts of peach mixture over each tartlet. Top with 2 tablespoons
ice cream. Serve warm or at room temperature.

Exchanges
1 1/2 Fat
2 1/2 Carbohydrate

Calories 254
  Calories from Fat 103
Total Fat .... 11 g
  Saturated Fat .... 5 g
Cholesterol .... 19 mg
Sodium .... 157 mg
Carbohydrate .... 35 g
  Dietary Fiber .... 1 g
  Sugars .... 14 g
Protein .... 3 g

Sticky Maple Pecan Pull-Aparts

Serves: 8

Serving size:
1 pull-apart

1 11-ounce container refrigerated French
bread dough
2 tablespoons reduced-fat margarine
2 tablespoons sugar
2 teaspoons ground cinnamon
1/4 cup pure maple syrup or honey
(not pancake syrup)
1/2 cup chopped pecans

1 Preheat oven to 350°F.

2 Unfold dough on a work surface or cutting
board. Spread margarine evenly over entire
surface.

3 In a small bowl, combine sugar and cinnamon
and sprinkle evenly over all. Roll dough back up
and, using a serrated knife, gently cut into 8 pieces.

4 Pour syrup in an 8-inch nonstick baking pan
and tilt pan to coat bottom evenly. Sprinkle
nuts over syrup. Place rolls in pan, cut side down,
on top of the pecans and syrup.

5 Bake 30 minutes or until rolls sound hollow
when tapped lightly. Place serving plate on top
of rolls and invert. Scrape any remaining syrup and
nuts from pan and spoon on top of rolls. Serve
warm or at room temperature.

Exchanges
1 Fat
2 Carbohydrate

Calories 192
   Calories from Fat 65
Total Fat .... 7 g
   Saturated Fat .... 1 g
Cholesterol .... 0 mg
Sodium .... 252 mg
Carbohydrate .... 28 g
   Dietary Fiber .... 1 g
   Sugars .... 11 g
Protein .... 4 g

Serves: 9

Serving size:
  1 tablespoon plus
  1/2 cup fruit

Double Dark Mocha Chocolate Syrup

1/4 cup fat-free milk
  2 tablespoons light corn syrup
1 1/2 teaspoons instant coffee granules
  3 ounces semi-sweet chocolate chips
1/2 teaspoon vanilla
4 1/2 cups fruit of choice, such as banana slices,
    pineapple chunks, or strawberries

1 Place a small saucepan over medium heat. Add milk, corn syrup, and coffee granules and bring just to a simmer.

2 Remove from heat and stir in remaining ingredients until smooth. Let cool completely.

3 To serve, thread fruit on bamboo skewers or place in individual dessert dishes and drizzle chocolate sauce evenly over all.

Exchanges
1 1/2 Carbohydrate

Calories	104
Calories from Fat	28
Total Fat	3 g
Saturated Fat	2 g
Cholesterol	0 mg
Sodium	10 mg
Carbohydrate	21 g
Dietary Fiber	2 g
Sugars	16 g
Protein	1 g

Exchanges
(syrup only)
1/2 Fat
1/2 Carbohydrate

Calories	61
Calories from Fat	26
Total Fat	3 g
Saturated Fat	2 g
Cholesterol	0 mg
Sodium	10 mg
Carbohydrate	10 g
Dietary Fiber	1 g
Sugars	8 g
Protein	1 g

Cranberry-Pecan Baked Apples

Serves: 4

Serving size:
  1/4 recipe

1/4 cup pecan pieces
1/4 cup dried sweetened cranberries
1/2 teaspoon grated orange rind
1/2 teaspoon ground cinnamon
1/4 teaspoon ground nutmeg
  1 tablespoon reduced-fat margarine
  2 medium apples, such as Gala, halved and cored
  3 tablespoons orange juice
  1 tablespoon dark brown sugar, packed
1/2 teaspoon vanilla

1 Preheat oven to 400°F.

2 Coat a 9-inch pie pan with cooking spray and sprinkle pecans and cranberries over bottom of pan. Sprinkle nuts evenly with orange rind, cinnamon, and nutmeg. Dot with small amounts margarine evenly over all.

3 Pierce apple skin in several places with a fork and place (cut side down) on top of pecan mixture. Bake, uncovered, 20 minutes or until tender crisp.

4 Remove apples from pan and place on serving platter. Stir orange juice, sugar, and vanilla vigorously into pan drippings. Spoon topping over apples.

Exchanges
2 Fruit
1 1/2 Fat

Calories	171
Calories from Fat	64
Total Fat	7 g
Saturated Fat	1 g
Cholesterol	0 mg
Sodium	20 mg
Carbohydrate	29 g
Dietary Fiber	4 g
Sugars	23 g
Protein	1 g

Lemon Zest Pound Cake with Apricot Topping

1/4 cup flour
  1 box pound cake mix
    Grated rind of 1 medium lemon
3/4 cup water
1/2 cup egg substitute
1/2 cup apricot 100% fruit spread

1 Preheat oven to 350°F.

2 Coat two 8 1/2-inch × 4 1/2-inch loaf pans with cooking spray. Dust each pan with 2 tablespoons flour. Discard any remaining flour.

3 Combine cake mix, lemon rind, water, and egg substitute. Beat on low speed 30 seconds; beat on medium speed 3 minutes.

4 Pour batter into pans and bake 30 minutes or until wooden toothpick inserted comes out clean. Cool 10 minutes. Remove from pan and cool completely on wire rack.

5 Whisk fruit spread until pliable and spread 1/4 cup on each cake.

Exchanges

1/2 Fat
2 Carbohydrate

Calories 170
  Calories from Fat 36
Total Fat ....4 g
  Saturated Fat ....1 g
Cholesterol ....0 mg
Sodium ....133 mg
Carbohydrate ....33 g
  Dietary Fiber ....0 g
  Sugars ....19 g
Protein ....2 g

Index

SUBJECT INDEX

About the American Diabetes Association

The American Diabetes Association is the nation's leading voluntary health organization supporting diabetes research, information, and advocacy. Its mission is to prevent and cure diabetes and to improve the lives of all people affected by diabetes. The American Diabetes Association is the leading publisher of comprehensive diabetes information. Its huge library of practical and authoritative books for people with diabetes covers every aspect of self-care—cooking and nutrition, fitness, weight control, medications, complications, emotional issues, and general self-care.

To order American Diabetes Association books: Call 1-800-232-6733. Or log on to http://store.diabetes.org

To join the American Diabetes Association: Call 1-800-806-7801. www.diabetes.org/membership

For more information about diabetes or ADA programs and services: Call 1-800-342-2383. E-mail: Customerservice@diabetes.org or log on to www.diabetes.org

To locate an ADA/NCQA Recognized Provider of quality diabetes care in your area: www.ncqa.org/dprp/

To find an ADA Recognized Education Program in your area: Call 1-888-232-0822. www.diabetes.org/recognition/education.asp

To join the fight to increase funding for diabetes research, end discrimination, and improve insurance coverage: Call 1-800-342-2383. www.diabetes.org/advocacy

To find out how you can get involved with the programs in your community: Call 1-800-342-2383. See below for program Web addresses.

- *American Diabetes Month:* Educational activities aimed at those diagnosed with diabetes—month of November. www.diabetes.org/ADM
- *American Diabetes Alert:* Annual public awareness campaign to find the undiagnosed—held the fourth Tuesday in March. www.diabetes.org/alert
- *The Diabetes Assistance & Resources Program (DAR):* diabetes awareness program targeted to the Latino community. www.diabetes.org/DAR
- *African American Program:* diabetes awareness program targeted to the African American community. www.diabetes.org/africanamerican
- *Awakening the Spirit: Pathways to Diabetes Prevention & Control:* diabetes awareness program targeted to the Native American community. www.diabetes.org/awakening

To find out about an important research project regarding type 2 diabetes: www.diabetes.org/ada/research.asp

To obtain information on making a planned gift or charitable bequest: Call 1-888-700-7029. www.diabetes.org/ada/plan.asp

To make a donation or memorial contribution: Call 1-800-342-2383. www.diabetes.org/ada/cont.asp